Race, Class
and Conservatism

Race, Class and Conservatism

THOMAS D. BOSTON

Georgia Institute of Technology, Atlanta, Georgia

Boston

UNWIN HYMAN

London   Sydney   Wellington

Unwin Hyman, Inc.
8 Winchester Place, Winchester, Mass. 01890, USA

Published by the Academic Division of
Unwin Hyman Ltd
15/17 Broadwick Street, London W1V 1FP, UK

Allen & Unwin (Australia) Ltd,
8 Napier Street, North Sydney, NSW 2060, Australia

Allen & Unwin (New Zealand) Ltd in association with
the Port Nicholson Press Ltd,
60 Cambridge Terrace, Wellington, New Zealand

First Published in 1988

Library of Congress Cataloging-in-Publication Data

Boston, Thomas D.
    Race, class, and conservatism / Thomas D. Boston.
      p. cm.
    Bibliography: p.
    Includes index.
    ISBN 0–04–330368–4 (alk. paper).
          0–04–330369–2 (pbk. : alk. paper)
    1. Social classes—United States.
    2. United States—Race relations.
    3. Afro–Americans—Social conditions.
    4. Afro–Americans—Employment.
    5. Conservatism—United States.
I. Title
HN90.S6B67   1988   88–982
305.5'0973—dc 19   CIP

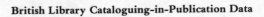

British Library Cataloguing-in-Publication Data

Boston, Thomas D.
    Race, class and conservatism.
    1. United States. Black persons. Economic conditions of effects. Social
class
I. Title
330.973'008996073
ISBN 0-04-330368-4
          0-04-330369-2 (pbk)

Typeset in 10 on 12 point Bembo
Printed in Great Britain by Billing and Sons Ltd, London and Worcester

Contents

CONTENTS

Figures

Tables

Acknowledgements

I greatly appreciate the tremendous support provided by the publisher's staff and affiliates. In particular I would like to thank the Editor, Gordon Smith, for his patience and assistance, the former Economics Editor Walter Allen and Professor Edward Nell. Writing for Unwin Hyman Ltd. has been a pleasurable experience. In a draft version of some initial research for this project, I received very helpful comments from Sandy Darity, Paul Sweezy, Harry Magdoff, Anna Willman and Lynn Burbridge. I am also deeply indebted to Gary Dymski for initially proposing the undertaking and providing valuable editorial comments all throughout.

Donald Harris arranged for me to spend a sabbatical at the Department of Economics, Stanford University, during 1983 and 1984. This afforded a rare opportunity to discuss these ideas both with Don and with St Clair Drake, and to receive comments from John Gurley. During the same period Professor Zhang Shu Zhi invited me to lecture on race and class at the Department of Economics, Shanghai Institute of Finance and Economics, People's Republic of China. I will always remember the insightful comments of the faculty and students of the institute, and their warm hospitality.

I do not have space to mention their names, but this research was greatly inspired by the dozens of students who enrolled in my political economy classes at Atlanta University. Their thrust for understanding and criticisms of old ideas made me search constantly for new solutions. This book was largely written at Georgia Institute of Technology, and there are several individuals whose assistance and support I must acknowledge. I thank Richard Henderson and Mark Gravitt for assistance with the *Current Population Survey*, Fred Tarpley and Dean Jerry Day for a wealth of resource support and Margaret Pirl and Nancy Stubbins for valuable research assistance.

Finally, I am most grateful to my wife Catherine Ross for a reservoir of support, patience and constructive critiques. This was priceless.

Introduction

Race, Class and Conservatism addresses several of the most pressing issues of our times. It investigates the historical roots and contemporary manifestations of racial economic inequality, examines sociologically the internal structure of class stratification in black society and rebuts the central propositions of neoconservative economists on the role of racial discrimination in black economic advancement.

The arguments contained herein are a response to five recent controversial books: William J. Wilson's *Declining Significance of Race* (1978), Thomas Sowell's *Markets and Minorities* (1981) and *Civil Rights: Rhetoric or Reality?* (1984), George Gilder's *Wealth and Poverty* (1981) and Walter Williams's *State against Blacks* (1982). This book opposes the conclusions derived in those investigations. In essence, they contend that the disadvantaged position of blacks in American society cannot be attributed to racial discrimination.

In examining the issues, we have attempted to go beyond simply providing contrary evidence and offer instead alternative explanations of dynamics involved. For example, when investigating the relative impact of race and class on black economic opportunity, we start by defining class, identifying the nature of stratification in black society, locating its changes over time and finally highlighting its interaction with racial dynamics. This in itself is a major undertaking. Additionally, while rebutting conservative denials of discrimination, we demonstrate how it persists and is perpetuated through segmented labor markets.

These findings will not be received comfortably by conservatives because they are just another chapter in the continuing saga of why their 'revolution' has failed so miserably. Flawed theory creates failed policies. By the way, where are the supply-side economists? This group, which once loudly proclaimed itself to be 'the best friend of the poor in America' (Gilder, 1981, p. xiv), has disappeared. And what about the chaos left behind? If asked to give the briefest possible description of the outcome of their policies, it would be as follows. *Never have so few said so little and disordered so much.* Does discrimination exist in contemporary labor markets, and if so how? Is class station more important than racial inequity in determining the social advancement of blacks? Our response to these two central questions can be summarized briefly. First, discrimination persists, but is expressed primarily by differences in relative black/white employment opportunities and occupational status as opposed to wage inequalities. Secondly, class station is important, but black class stratification itself has been determined largely by race.

Leaving aside for a moment the merits of the arguments, which can only be decided by time and subjection to scholarly scrutiny, there is another ingredient of the investigation that is important. This is its methodological approach. To address the issues properly, they must first be placed within an appropriate methodological framework. The one we have chosen is best illustrated by a careful reading of the table of contents.

This book evolved out of four earlier activities: first, a series of class lectures given while on the faculty of Atlanta University; second, an article prepared for the *Review of Radical Political Economics*, special issue on Race and Class (Boston, 1985); third, a lecture given at the Shanghai Institute of Finance and Economics, People's Republic of China; finally, it draws upon my experiences in the Civil Rights Movement. As such, I am deeply indebted to many individuals.

In most cases, I have tried to avoid using the jargon of economics and other disciplines in order to make the book more digestible to a general audience. At times this proved impossible – as for example in developing the arguments on class definitions and stratification, and in proving the existence of discrimination through regression and logit analyses. Nevertheless, these are extremely minor aspects of the overall presentation and mainly provide supporting evidence. The book opens with an outline of the arguments and debates of conservative economists. Their central hypotheses are identified, along with the line of our counter-argument. After establishing this, the remaining chapters are devoted to a detailed investigation of the validity of each proposition.

Supply-side economics is dead, and its boastful promises have not been realized. Further, the moderate economic growth we have experienced over the last several years has come at the expense of the economy being burdened by a budget deficit of historic proportions, record trade imbalances, gyrating financial markets, declining real incomes and a diminishing safety net for the poor. Worse still, these developments were preceded by the steepest recession in postwar history. Still, some blacks have embraced the conservative agenda. Thomas Sowell and Walter Williams are perhaps the most quoted in this regard. Their theories are grounded in the philosophies of classical economics and became key ingredients of the short-lived supply-side revolution. Although the latter has disintegrated completely, its theories pertaining to blacks have outlived the revolution and are still integral to current government policies.

Along with supply-side policies, the entire conservative agenda is crumbling so rapidly it may not survive Reaganism. Beneath the surface of free market Darwinism, a growing disenchantment has emerged. Jobs, peace, poverty, the homeless and racial justice are themes of the 1990s. But haunted by the failures of supply-side economics and entrapped by ideological purity, the new conservative cannot address these issues and as such is slowly becoming a political dinosaur.

1 Race, Class and Conservatism: the Issues and the Debate

For more than a century the relation of race and class in American society has been an enigma to social scientists. At the turn of the century the topic was addressed in W. E. B. Dubois's examination of *The Philadelphia Negro* (1899). Decades later Allison Davis's *Deep South* (1941), Gunnar Myrdal's *An American Dilemma* (1944) and E. Franklin Frazier's *Black Bourgeoisie* (1957) captured national attention. Still, today this topic is at the center of a passionate controversy. With the publication of William J. Wilson's *Declining Significance of Race* (1978) and several treatises by Thomas Sowell, including *Markets and Minorities* (1981), a new hypothesis is presented. It asserts that class position instead of racial discrimination is the determining factor in the present status and future opportunities of blacks.

> Race relations in America have undergone fundamental changes in recent years, so much so that now the life chances of individual blacks have more to do with their economic class position than with their day-to-day encounters with whites.
>
> (Wilson, 1978, p. 1)

Although Wilson is not a conservative, his hypothesis, along with those of Sowell (1981, 1984) and Williams (1982b), constitutes the foundation of neoconservative ideas on race.[1] This view contends that racial discrimination has all but vanished and can no longer be blamed for impeding the progress of black society. To the contrary, the lower endowment of education and skills possessed

1

by blacks, affirmative action programs, government intervention in free markets, civil rights politics and black social and cultural deficiencies, are impediments to social advancement.

> Racial bigotry and discrimination is neither a complete nor satisfactory explanation for the *current* condition of many blacks in America . . . instead of racial discrimination and bigotry, it is the 'rules of the game' that account for many of the economic handicaps faced by blacks. The rules of the game are the many federal, state and local laws that regulate economic activity.
>
> (Williams, 1982b, p. xv)

Departing radically from traditional thinking, conservatives assert that it is both theoretically and practically impossible for free markets to sustain racial discrimination. The differential costs associated with practicing discrimination in a competitive market, they assert, will drive into bankruptcy any firm engaging in racially motivated hiring and compensation (Block and Walker, 1982, p. xvi). Their most fundamental hypothesis contends that discrimination is mainly illusory and disappears almost completely when one controls for differences in human capital endowment and class positions between blacks and whites. The reasoning is as follows. Measures of racial discrimination and inequality are flawed because they do not adequately account for differences between blacks and whites in occupation, quality of education, degree of job experience, individual initiative, stability of family structure, age and fertility rates, or for differences in geographical dispersion among ethnic groups. While most apparent income discrimination will disappear once these factors are controlled, that which remains can be explained by the greater concentration of blacks among the lower class and the deficiencies in culture generated thereby. As Gilder argues: 'Many apparent manifestations of racial and ethnic prejudice, for example, are in fact expressions of economic class – the natural reluctance of higher classes to expose their children to lower-class values' (1981, p. 90).

It is apparent now why Wilson's hypothesis is both so necessary and compelling to conservatives. In neoclassical analyses of racial

2

income inequality, one controls for human capital factors, and the unexplained differences in income between blacks and whites constitute discrimination. To conservatives this residual difference reflects not discrimination but the so-called social pathologies, family instability and low-achievement ethos of the underclass. As such, class location rather than racial discrimination accounts for residual income differences. Besides, they claim, everyone should know and agree that in a competitive free market system class status is based solely upon one's individual initiative – or lack thereof. One dare not speak of race as a determining feature of this impersonal process.

My contention is precisely the opposite! First, discrimination does not disappear when one controls for human capital and demographic differences between races. Secondly, the disproportionate representation of blacks among the lower-classes is itself a product of racial discrimination. Indeed, the entire black class structure has been distorted by the historic and contemporary practices of racial subordination in American society. These issues constitute the central focus of the present study.

Over the last two decades, a growing black minority have made significant progress, while an even larger segment of workers have become increasingly marginalized. This has led Wilson and others to conclude that class is more important than race. But where Wilson admits that racism still persists in social institutions, conservatives are not so inclined. Highlighting the convergence between the upper tiers of the black and white class structures, and attributing the absence of convergence among the black lower class to cultural or human capital deficiencies, they dismiss almost completely racial discrimination as a causal factor. It is therefore imperative that we grapple once again with this perplexing question of race and class in contemporary society.

Current studies of race and class, even those not embracing the conservative position, have four fundamental shortcomings. First, the stratification of classes, that is, the very entity under consideration, is inaccurately defined. Second, the internal structure of each class is completely ignored. The mean progress of the class is usually discussed: even the growing divergence between upper and lower classes. But the dichotomous development of internal class sub-groupings is neglected, and it is here that the historical

3

and contemporary impact of racial discrimination is clearest. Third, a pervasive problem is the rigidity of approaches. Most authors assert that the status of black society is determined by either race or class, without an explanation of the interaction between the two. The debate by Clark and Gershman (1980) is typical in this regard. Finally, they fail to grasp fully the historic role of race in forming and regenerating the disarticulated class configuration of black society.

These errors are analytically crippling. But given the logic of the conservative argument, the last omission is particularly serious. Historically, racial subjugation has created a unique class stratification, reflecting the inferior economic position blacks have been forced to occupy. This inferior status is constantly regenerated not only by economic dynamics, but also by the legal, cultural, political and social apparatuses which support it. Hence, even when racism is removed fully from laws, it lingers in other aspects of society's superstructure and economic substructure. Furthermore, it is vividly reflected in the quantitative and qualitative differences between black and white class structures.

Contemporary class inequality is the product of a history of racial inequality. For example, assume that a system of 'Jim Crow' relegates blacks disproportionately to the status of sharecroppers, and suddenly such segregation is declared illegal. Is Jim Crowism no longer a factor in the life chances of blacks, even though they are still sharecroppers? One cannot maintain this until the inferior economic status created by Jim Crow is abolished. But any set of production relations, once institutionalized, is regenerated over a reasonably long period of time. There is an analogous situation today. Therefore, *if conservatives believe that differences in class position and human capital attributes account overwhelmingly for racial income differences, we must remind them constantly that the black class structure and human capital accumulation are themselves functions of racial subordination.*[2]

In this and the subsequent chapter, we undertake an investigation of black class structure which corrects these flaws. Our principal hypotheses are twofold. First, the Civil Rights era, just as earlier periods of intense black political activity, brought about significant changes in the internal structure of black social classes. In fact, the new black conservative, a complementary component of the conservative consensus sweeping mainstream politics in America, is tied closely to a stratum of the new black middle class whose ascendancy, ironically, dates from the Civil Rights era. Second, despite these changes racial subordination has been, and continues to be, intrinsic in determining the structure of black classes and hence in explaining the extent of social and economic inequality vis-a-vis white society. It goes without saying that one must first adequately define classes before their stratification and relations can be examined.

We shall see that enormous quantitative and qualitative differences between black and white class structures still exist; and such differences are products of racial subordination. Therefore, conservative arguments which deny a determining role for race must be rejected in favor of views which acknowledge the continued presence of racial discrimination as a key factor in the life chances of black society.

Difficulties in Defining Class

Investigations of race and class are difficult – particularly given the immense social and economic changes taking place in American society. Leaving aside race, the concept of class has been referred to as an 'intellectual jellyfish' (Pryor, 1981, p. 369). Yet Parkin reminds us:

> Now that racial, ethnic, and religious conflicts have moved towards the center of the political stage in many industrial societies, any general model of class or stratification that does not fully incorporate this fact must forfeit all credibility.
>
> (1979, p. 9)

But researchers have still not adequately incorporated race in class analyses. Part of the reason for this omission is the mistaken belief that industrial societies dissolve all ethnic differences. Parkin attributes the problem also to the adoption of a certain methodology within which ethnic factors become '"complicating features" that simply disturb the pure class model, rather than as integral elements of the system' (1979, p. 32).

5

Three major issues are involved in class analyses. These are as follows. (1) The need to define or identify the boundaries of the basic classes; more specifically, we must determine the factors which are responsible for constituting certain segments of the population into a social class as distinct from other segments. Included in this is the need to understand the problems presented by the intersection or overlap of certain class characteristics. Overlapping characteristics often give the impression that criteria used to define a class are not unique but are found also among members of another class. (2) The necessity to identify correlations between classes and forms of ideological and political consciousness. And (3) the need to analyze the interaction between racial subordination and class composition and determine the impact of the existing class configuration on general economic and social development. While each of these issues is difficult, little progress can be made until classes are sufficiently defined: a task which has proven elusive.

Today, definitions of class vary widely, but the two most prominent are the Weberian and the Marxian. In the latter approach classes are defined by the ownership relation to the means of production and conceived as dynamic agents of social change. Within the Weberian conception, they are status groupings defined by a common set of socioeconomic relations and life chances. Added to these are approaches which stratify classes by occupational categories, income levels and power relations.

Most contemporary analyses of black classes employ the Weberian method. This procedure looks primarily to market relations as the basis for class divisions. Weber states:

> We may speak of a class when (1) a number of people have in common a specific causal component of their life chances, insofar as (2) this component is represented exclusively by economic interests in the possession of goods and opportunities for income, and (3) is represented under the conditions of the commodity or labor markets. This is 'class situation.'
>
> (Weber, 1978, p. 927)

Usually, such approaches are combined with stratifications based upon occupational categories. For example, Landry defines

6

classes as 'groups differing from each other by the average market situation or rewards of the positions their members occupy.' He further suggests that a minimum distinction be made between manual and non-manual or white-collar and blue-collar workers (1980, p. 3). Similarly, Wilson (1978, p. ix) defines a class as 'any group of people who have more or less similar goods, services, or skills to offer for income in a given economic order and who therefore receive similar financial remuneration in the marketplace.' Modifying Frazier's (1957) approach, Wilson identifies the black middle class as those employed in white-collar jobs, craftsmen and those in foreman positions.

There are several problems common to most analyses of black stratification. The first and most serious involves mis-specifying class boundaries. For example, researchers typically merge the black capitalist class with the black middle class: as if they constitute only one class. The small size of the former is usually the rationale. However, this practice leads to serious conceptual omissions. Since Reconstruction, there has existed a black capitalist class, despite its extremely weak state. Rather than overlooking it, the historical conditions responsible for maintaining its feeble existence are important issues for analysis. In fact, the weak state of the black capitalist is a major aspect of modern racial inequality.

The black capitalist is the victim of a long history of illegal property expropriation and financial discrimination, and for many decades a legalized system of racial segregation. These facts help explain why there exists today a capitalist class of only a few thousand out of a total black population of over 26 million – see Figure 1.1. As we shall see, this issue is fundamental to understanding the historical roots of black inequality.

Two additional errors of mis-specification involve the tendency to classify the middle class arbitrarily by an income boundary. Such approaches typically place all people making $25,000 or more in the middle or upper class. A second problem involves the concept of the 'black underclass,' where the latter is never defined precisely. We are generally led to believe this underclass consists primarily of black female-headed households and pathological misfits. These two characteristics are attributed with a vicious circle of self-perpetuating poverty which constantly regenerates the underclass. But the economic dynamics that produce the

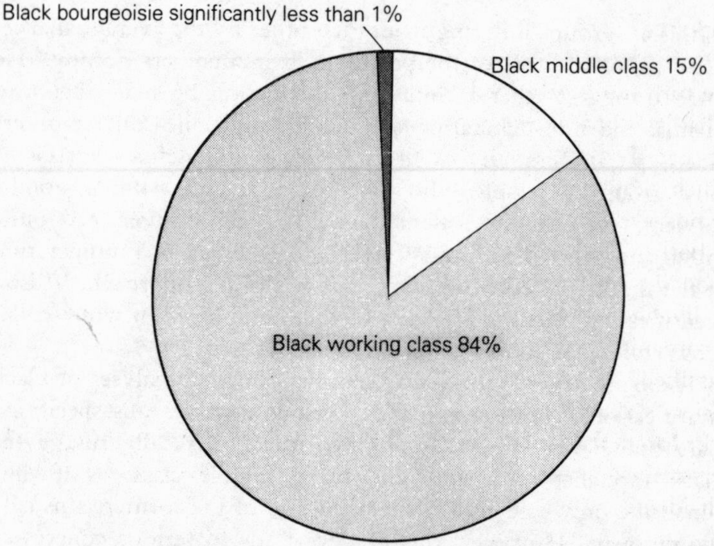

Black bourgeoisie significantly less than 1%

Black middle class 15%

Black working class 84%

Figure 1.1 Relative proportions of black social classes.
Source: Based on discussion in Chapter 2.

underclass are never examined. Instead the impression is given that this stratum exists in isolation from the dynamics of the economy and polity and is responsible for its own impoverishment.

The whole issue of the black underclass is used cleverly by the conservative movement. The new emphasis on class, which was most clearly articulated in Wilson's *Declining Significance of Race* (1978), provided conservatives a fresh camouflage to hide their antipathy for social policies behind a concern for the growing class division in black society. But for a movement whose underlying ideology is not only elitist, but based also upon a presumption of 'trickle down' (Gilder, 1981), it is very interesting that their major criticism of black leadership, affirmative action and other government policies has to do with the stagnation of the black underclass. To a person, conservatives pretend to have a great compassion for the black underclass – a concern which fits conveniently within their nexus of attack on liberal policies. Liberals, they assert, are responsible for the stagnation. Yet black poverty and unemployment have been particularly grievous under the current conservative administration.

Defining Class

We turn now to the tedious but necessary task of defining class.[3] What is a class? Social consciousness, political actions and inactions are greatly influenced by the institutional arrangements within which people earn their means of livelihood. Such influences may be positive or negative. Further, location within these institutions is both voluntarily and involuntarily determined and depends upon the extent to which each person controls his or her means of livelihood. Social classes are a common denominator used to organize these objective and subjective arrangements. Once classified, the results should reveal some useful information on society's development.

Pryor defines class as the designation of a group into which persons are placed by either objective criteria, subjective criteria, self-identification, or mixed criteria.

> Depending upon the theory of social stratification that is proposed, 'class' can be defined in terms of 'objective' criteria (e.g. income, wealth, position), 'subjective' criteria (solidarity in terms of social or economic interests; or self-identification with some group) or mixed criteria (e.g. evaluation by others in society in terms of esteem or some other scale of value). Depending upon the theory of social structure that is proposed, 'class' can be defined in terms of a group that is struggling together to change the structure; or statistically in terms of the position or power of the group concerning the operations of the society in equilibrium. Depending upon the theory of societal causation that is proposed, 'class' can embrace a difference defined in terms of a single criterion or of some combination or set of criteria.
>
> (Pryor, 1981, pp. 369–70)

Economists of the classical era, such as Adam Smith, David Ricardo and Karl Marx, focused a great deal on the social implications of economic processes, and were quite comfortable using class as an analytical tool. Their definitions were based on objective criteria which viewed class as a station emanating from one's position in the economic hierarchy, functional role in the organization of production, ownership of the means of production, or lack thereof. Today, such objective criteria are associated with the Marxian approach. To Horowitz the unique feature of the Marxian approach

9

is not the idea of class but rather the concept of class struggle or specifically class as an instrument of political transformation. This is synonymous with the distinction commonly made between 'a class acting as an objective entity in its own right' and a class 'acting in a subjective way for its own right' (1979, p. 55). Most contemporary notions of class have been criticized precisely because they cannot identify a collective interest or subjective behaviour peculiar to class members.

One unique element introduced into the discussion by Weber is the idea that economic opportunity or life chances, rather than economic station, binds classes together. Specifically, the behavior of classes is determined as much by values and common circumstances as by position in the social hierarchy (Horowitz, 1979, p. 55; see also Weber, 1978, p. 927). But if one of the principal objectives of class theory is to identify the main social cleavage, or as Parkin says 'the structural "fault" running through society to which the most serious disturbances on the political landscape are thought to be ultimately traceable' (1979, p. 3), then Weberian analysis is clearly lacking. Its most obvious shortcoming is the inability to identify class boundaries clearly: a problem traceable to its focus on the distribution system and status groups as opposed to production relations. In short, one may identify several sets of common values and circumstances. On the other hand, the theory's strength is its recognition that individuals sharing common life chances and circumstances tend to share ideological outlooks.

The Marxian method is built on a more objective foundation because boundaries are derived from ownership relations to the means of production. In this approach social classes are

large groups of people differing from each other by the place they occupy in a historically determined system of social production, by their relation (in most cases fixed and formulated by law) to the means of production, by their role in the social organization of labour, and, consequently, by the dimensions of the share of social wealth of which they dispose and the mode of acquiring it. Classes are groups of people one of which can appropriate the labour of another owing to the different places they occupy in a definite system of social economy.

(Lenin, 1974, p. 421)

The definition embodies three elements: (1) the relations of individuals to the ownership of the means of production; (2) the division of labor and functions in the production process; and (3) the method of acquiring income and the pattern of its distribution. The first factor is considered to be most important in determining class formations.

Unlike the Weberian method, boundaries in the Marxian approach are more definitive. However, the method often experiences difficulty in attempting to correlate ideological and political attitudes with objective class locations. For example, a well-known and frequently encountered problem is the incongruence of workers' class actions with their class station. Secondly, the difficulty of deriving objective class boundaries has not been completely resolved, especially given the changing structures of advanced industrial economies. Is there a new ruling class now that 'family capitalism' has disappeared and ownership is divorced from control of production? Similarly, with the growing importance of information technology, service industries, financial services and the like, the classical industrial proletariat is disappearing. Does this mean there now exists a new middle class or a new working class? These are complex issues which have not been resolved fully.

Neither the Marxian nor the Weberian method has sufficiently resolved the boundary problem. The greater advantage displayed by the Weberian method in correlating consciousness with status groupings is offset by the limitless number of such groups that may be identified. Hence its boundary problem is very severe. On the other hand, the Marxian method has been plagued by the opposite problem, that of correlating boundaries to class consciousness. Finally, neither method accounts properly for complexities that arise when racial divisions are introduced (Parkin, 1979, p. 4).

We repeat, the major problem of class analysis is the boundary problem. To put this into better focus, Figure 1.2, illustrating class boundaries and intersections, has been constructed. Assume the bell-shaped curves represent the boundaries or characteristics used to identify individuals of classes A and B. Whatever defining characteristics we select, it is obvious that there will exist some variation in the degree to which these characteristics are possessed by members of both classes. For the sake of argument we assume that possession of the relevant characteristics by class members is normally distributed about a mean. At the tails of the distributions

11

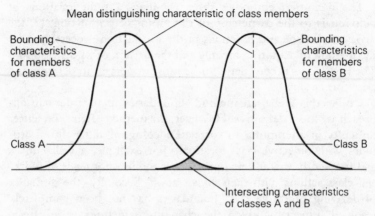

Figure 1.2 Class boundaries and intersections.

this variation is large and creates much of the confusion in regard to defining boundaries of classes.

As our areas of intersection illustrate, it is possible and logical that individuals of class A possess some characteristics of members of class B; yet, in a fundamental sense, they are still members of A. For example, the income and lifestyle of some workers will exceed those of some middle-class professionals. Yet we should not reclassify the professional or worker simply on the basis of income. Otherwise, an entrepreneur who runs in the red one year would automatically become a worker, which is nonsensical. Yet such intersecting lifestyle and income characteristics are always prevalent and create obvious problems when defining classes, distinguishing boundaries and attempting to correlate consciousness with class location. Authors of various persuasions, including Marxian, liberal and conservative, have attempted with greater or lesser degrees of success to resolve this problem (Bell, 1973, 1975, 1979; Giddens, 1973; Giddens and Mackenzie, 1982; Horowitz, 1979; Kristol, 1978; Poulantzas, 1973, 1975; Pryor, 1981; Wright, 1978, 1979).

Perhaps Sweezy captures best the notion of overlapping characteristics by asserting:

It would be a mistake to think of a class as perfectly homogeneous internally and sharply marked off from other classes. Actually, there is variety within the class; and one class sometimes shades off very gradually and almost imperceptibly

12

into another. We must, therefore, think of the class as being made up of a core surrounded by fringes which are in varying degrees attached to the core. A fringe may be more or less stable and have a well-defined function in relation to the class as a whole, or it may be temporary and accidental.

(1953, p. 124)

A good part of the definition and boundary problem in class analyses would be resolved if researchers recognized that over-lapping characteristics are perfectly normal, instead of attempting to define impermeable boundaries. The object then is to build definitions incorporating this fact rather than skirt it with rigid and unrealistic assumptions.

The 'New Class'

Another roadblock to the advance of class analysis is the concept of the 'new class.' We have become so accustomed to this expression that its existence is accepted almost axiomatically. Some authors claim that there is a new ruling class of managers or public administrators which has displaced the traditional capitalist class of property owners. Others contend that a new middle class of knowledge workers has emerged and consists of scientists, technicians, academicians and on occasion all white-collar workers. Generally the discussion of a 'new class' centers on four relatively new social developments: (1) the divorce of ownership from management and control of the corporation; (2) the increasing technological base of modern industry; (3) the growth of the service sector relative to the manufacturing sector; and (4) the increasing share of the total economy falling under the control of the government and public administrators. This last point has been very important in propelling conservatives vigorously into the class debate. 'Big government' runs counter to their free market philosophy, and they believe it reflects liberal ideas and influences.

In recent social science literature, the concept of a 'New Class' is often invoked but variously defined. Roughly speaking, it comprises the educated white collar workers who do not own the physical means of production but who nevertheless act as a potent political and economic force through their intellectual activities,

13

either as decision-makers in industry and in government or in the nonmarket sector and/or as definers and transmitters of new ideological forces. The class has arisen as a result of three major forces: mass education; an increasing level of economic development which has been accompanied by a rise in the relative importance of a highly educated white collar labor force (as staff, symbol manipulators, or scientists); and a decline in the traditional ideological support of capitalism as ownership has been separated from control and as entrepreneurship has been bureaucratized.

(Pryor, 1981, p. 367)

The separation of ownership from management and control was recognized by Burnham in *The Managerial Revolution*; because of this, he asserts, a new social class – the managers – has grown to supremacy (1941, p. 74). Further, as businesses come under greater public ownership, government administrators have become increasingly dominant (Hacker, 1979, p. 49).

While top-level managers are thought to comprise the new ruling class, membership criteria in the new middle class are more ambiguous. Pryor (1981, pp. 370-1) summarizes several conceptions of the 'new class' including Gouldner (1979), Konrad and Szelenyi (1979) and Kristol (1978). His conclusions are that Gouldner believes that the new class consists of humanistic intellectuals and the technical intelligentsia. Second, that Konrad and Szelenyi define it as the stratum between workers and capitalists, with the core consisting of those with university educations. Finally, Pryor summarizes Kristol's view of the new class. This view holds that the new class consists of

college-educated individuals in occupations such as scientists, lawyers, city planners, social workers, educators, criminologists, sociologists, public health doctors, journalists and others in the media, psychologists, staffs of larger foundations, and the upper level of government bureaucracy who find their careers and/or economic interests in an expanding public sector.

(Pryor, 1981, p. 370)

Poulantzas provides the most ambitious Marxian attempt to delineate the class status of top-level administrators who manage institutions of government and corporations but do not share significantly in the corporation's ownership. He argues that managers

14

who share in the 'possession' but not the economic ownership of the means of production are part of the capitalist class, along with individuals who manage the apparatuses of government – for example, judicial, political, cultural and security institutions (1973, 1975; see also Wright, 1978, ch. 2).[4] On the other hand, supervisors are dominated by owners and managers but exercise control over workers. As such, he places the latter in the new middle class. Also included in the latter class are non-value-producing (that is, nonmanufacturing) workers. Membership in the working class is then reserved for the 'proletariat' as classically defined by Marx. Their labor alone, Poulantzas argues, is considered to be productive.[5]

Wright also addresses the issue of intersecting class characteristics, labelling such positions contradictory class locations. Although not stated explicitly, his analysis implies that such locations are new classes or at least quasi-classes. He argues that managers, who are excluded from any economic ownership but retain possession of the means of production, occupy a 'contradictory' or ambiguous position in the social hierarchy between capitalists and workers. Likewise semi-autonomous wage earners such as engineers and technicians occupy another contradictory class location (1978, p. 63).

It is argued that the new class must have a collective interest, the absence of which would indicate it is not truly a class. Some view its interest in an expanded public sector, feeling it benefits from increases in the state's jurisdiction and power. Horowitz is critical of the theory because it cannot predict social behavior. Is the new class more Republican or Democratic, liberal or conservative? he asks. 'Precisely the inability to make grandiose inferences from membership to behavior represents the Achilles heel among new-class theorists' (1979, p. 56). While some assert that it is generally more left-leaning because it has been educated in social criticism, Kristol contends that neoconservatism is the real and correct ideology of the new class (Pryor, 1981, p. 375).

A Synthesis

A major error in theories of the 'new class' is that authors describe it as a separate and distinct class. Contrary to this, we interpret 'new classes' as segments (fractions) or sub-groupings of existing classes.[6] When conceived as describing separate and distinct classes, 'new class' theories encounter the same major problem as tradition-al theories; they are unable to distinguish boundaries clearly. But conceived as describing segments of classes, this problem is more easily addressed.

To resolve the boundary issue we propose a synthesis which is unique because it attempts to combine several approaches to interpret class stratification. We draw upon and integrate aspects of class theory developed by Marx, Weber, Poulantzas and Giddens. If the approach seems eclectic, it is because the interpretation is derived by tailoring theories to fit reality rather than forcing reality into a preexisting class theory, and the appropriateness of the method should be judged by the extent to which the synthesis allows us to understand, explain and predict social reality.

To delineate the boundary of each class we rely on an individual's relationship to the ownership of the means of production: a Marxian method. But several modifications are made to this. First, we attempt to demonstrate the interplay of race with economics, politics and ideology in class composition. Second, the most important aspect of the analysis is its focus on the internal structure of classes, called their segments and strata: an approach emphasized by Poulantzas. But where Poulantzas failed to define segments (fractions) rigorously, we do so by drawing upon Weber's notion of life chances derived from the possession of goods and opportunities for income as a basic definition. Combining Weber's definition (which is related to the process of distribution) with an individual's location within the division of labor (a more objective and functional criterion) we derive a definition of a class segment – which in one sense is closely related to Weber's notion of a status group. A segment is a class sub-grouping comprised of individuals sharing common life chances derived from their similarities in income and functional roles within the division of labor. Further, each class can be decomposed into strata. These consist of individuals within a class who share common ideological, political and social orientations. In fact, strata are defined by the character of these ideological orientations. More importantly, we expect there to exist a significant correlation between a segment and a given stratum. This relationship is depicted in Figure 1.3.

16

Finally, we rely upon Giddens's method to explain the origin of the new middle class. But one difference we make is to interpret this development as a new segment of an existing middle class as opposed to a separate and distinct new class.

In our approach there exist three classes in society today: a capitalist class, a middle class and a working class. The capitalist class consists of individuals having ownership, control, or possession of the means of production and thereby the capacity to impact the livelihood of large numbers of workers. While the old segment of the capitalist class has ownership of the means of production, the new segment consists of individuals such as senior managers, executives and government officials having possession but not ownership of the instruments of production. While the

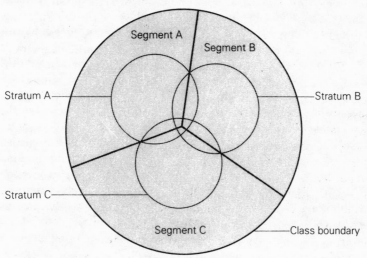

Class boundary: defined by one's ownership relation to the means of production.

Class segment: a sub-grouping within a class or a status grouping of individuals having similar 'life chances' derived from common locations within the division of labor and common patterns of income distribution.

Class stratum: defined by its political consciousness and social orientation. Significantly correlated with a particular segment.

Note: Our approach to class combines the methods of Marx, Weber, Poulantzas and Giddens.

Figure 1.3 The internal composition of a social class.

balance of power between the old and new capitalist segments still fundamentally favors the old, it may differ for any given social situation. Consider the recent shake-up at CBS Inc., where the powerful Chairman and Chief Executive Officer (who was not a principal owner) was dismissed (*Wall Street Journal*, 12 September 1986). This serves to illustrate an important point. Management has become separated from ownership; but ownership confers a right, while management, no matter how powerful, is a function (Bell, 1979, p. 20). Rulership resides ultimately in ownership. Yet it cannot be denied that managers are a new and powerful segment of the capitalist class.

The working class consists of individuals who do not own or control the means of production and must sell their labor to earn a living. This means also that it does not own the products of its labor (Marx, 1967, pp. 184-5). We exclude from the working class individuals whose laboring skills are so scarce that the possessor can command extraordinarily high wages or salaries in remuneration. Such individuals – for example, scientists, engineers and technicians – sell their labor but are not a part of the working class. Instead we classify them as the new middle class: a new segment of the middle class. We will have more to say on this point later. But for now we should acknowledge that Giddens (1973) introduced the idea that the possession of scarce forms of labor power can lead to the formation of a new middle class.

Finally, we address the status of individuals whose functional roles in society bring them into conflict with members of their origin class. For example, foremen are drawn from the ranks of workers and by income, lifestyle and all other measures are indistinguishable from the latter. But their responsibilities as foremen place them, in times of labor conflict, on the side of owners and managers. This is a typical example of how class consciousness can conflict with class station. Should we consider them workers even though their responsibilities in the division of labor conflict with the interests of workers? We contend that they are workers by origin but appended by function to the property-owning class, and the later aspect overrides the former. As appendages they are attached to and serve the interests of owners and managers but are not part of the capitalist class. In fact, this appendage status is made clear when, upon demotion, they typically resume their station as part of a lower class.

What then is the role of production and technology in class composition? The level of economic development, of which the productive forces are a part, plays an important role in establishing limits on the types of class that exist at any given historical period. For example, the slave economy prescribed a particular class configuration just as modern industry does. It is inconceivable that the class configuration of slave society could be compatible with today's level of industry and technology. But we cannot let our theoretical conception of class rest at simply defining boundaries, otherwise the examination will exist at a very abstract level.

To complete the analysis, the internal structure of each class must be specified: that is, the segments and strata. While industry and technology constrain the types of class that exist at any given time, political, social and for our purposes racial considerations shape the internal structure of classes. Further, these factors do not operate within a vacuum. But there is a continuous interaction between politics, economics and social development which dynamically affects the internal and external class structure.[7] We reject any notion of a deterministic relation between levels of production and class composition. Technology does not create classes; history does. Technology only *makes possible* the existence or dissolution of class configurations. In Chapter 2 we shall see how racial domination and resistance have interacted with each particular economic arrangement to alter the internal structure of black social classes.

Let us formally summarize the theoretical synthesis. The level of economic development is compatible with the existence of certain class stratifications and incompatible with others – hence those that are incompatible are dissolved in favor of the former. This is what we mean by saying the economy constrains the types of class that exist and it contrasts with the idea that the productive forces create certain classes.

In societies based on competitive capitalism we can identify class boundaries by examining the ownership pattern of the means of production. Having identified class boundaries we examine next the internal structure of each class. This consists of segments and strata, and we expect strata to be correlated with class segments. But the notion of a simple one-to-one correspondence between them must be rejected. Indeed, it should be anticipated that some individuals sharing common economic places and life chances will differ in their political orientation. After all, we are describing social and not mechanical interactions. The critical point is that there must exist a correlation, or significant intersection, between the two. Otherwise, the entire analysis is useless, and one could just as easily speak of classes defined by an income threshold. This latter approach would avoid the complications inherent in social class definitions, but would provide little by way of predicting political actions and social behavior. In summary, segments and strata constitute the internal structure of classes. Although often neglected, the subsequent analysis will reveal their critical importance in comprehending the relation of race and class in contemporary society.[8]

Notes: Chapter 1

1   While it is certainly not the case that all researchers subscribing to class explanations of black inequality are conservative, there is usually a large congruence in policy prescription between such advocates and conservatives.

2   Many shortcomings of conservative studies are shared by neoclassical and radical analyses. But at present I will focus on conservative approaches.

3   The remaining sections of this chapter are devoted to an exposition of class definitions and may be skipped with a minimal loss in continuity.

4   Poulantzas, 1975, p. 18, distinguishes economic ownership from possession of the instruments of production. The former refers to legal title or ownership as well as control over the productive process and the disposition of revenues generated thereby. Possession refers to control of the operations of production – a role reserved for managers.

5   For discussions of productive and nonproductive labor, see O'Connor, 1975; Mieksins, 1981; Resnick and Wolff, 1982.

6   The concept of a class segment is taken from Poulantzas, 1973, 1975, and is identical to his description of a 'fraction'. I refer to it as a segment instead of a fraction to make the presentation more palatable to the general readership.

7   A real challenge in class analysis is describing how internal structures change constantly in response to the polity and economy. In contrast external boundaries are relatively fixed, changing only over long periods of time. But at momentous historic periods, such as the Civil War in the USA, we do find external class relations changing swiftly.

8 While this examination of class structures is applicable to capitalist society in general, our subsequent analysis will reveal how it must be modified to account for the quantitative and qualitative differences in black class stratification created by a history of racial antagonisms.

2 Black Social Classes Today

Historically, racial conflict has interacted with economic, political and social arrangements to shape a unique stratification for blacks. To illustrate, we start by establishing the periods of black development and examine racial interaction and stratification during each period. Afterwards, the contemporary structure of black social classes is described. Wilson approaches the problem in a similar manner by identifying three stages of black/white interaction. He asserts: 'each stage embodies a different form of racial stratification structured by the particular arrangement of both the economy and the polity' (1978, p. 2). His first stage corresponds to the period of antebellum slavery and the early post-bellum era and is designated as the period of 'plantation economy and racial-caste oppression.' Stage two, ending with the New Deal era, is identified as 'industrial expansion, class conflict, and racial oppression.' Finally, stage three crystallized during the 1960s and 1970s and is the period of progressive transition from racial inequalities to class inequalities. In this latter period class supersedes race as the determining factor in the life chances of blacks (Wilson, 1978, pp. 2-3).

Our conception of Afro-American development is given in Figure 2.1. It identifies two main periods, each structured by the predominant production relation. Period I corresponds to the slavery era, while period II is characterized by free labor relations. Additionally, each period contains several stages. We have not identified the stages of period I, but for period II there are three: (1) black land tenancy, (2) the development of an urbanized wage labor force and (3) the current stage of increasing differentiation of black social classes. The latter is characterized by a progressive marginalization of black workers alongside the evolution of new segments of the black middle and capitalist classes. Stages and

22

Period I Slavery	Major transition era	Period II Free labor relations				
		Stage (1)	Minor Transition	Stage (2)	Minor transition	Stage (3)
Major event	Major events	Major event	Major events	Major event	Major events	Major events
Black enslavement in America	Civil War Forced labor Reconstruction Defeat of Reconstruction	Black land tenancy	Collapse of cotton tenancy Black out-migration from the South	Urbanized black labor force	Civil rights Economic stagnation Structural changes in the economy	Marginalization of black workers Evolution of new black middle class

Figure 2.1 Historical stages of Afro–American development.

periods are interspersed by transitions. Some transitions are major and alter the external relations of dominant and subordinate classes, as did the Civil War. Others, such as the collapse of cotton tenancy in the 1930s and the Civil Rights Movement of the 1960s, are minor and alter only the internal structure of classes.

The Civil War, the first transition, violently dismantled the slave system. According to Dubois, the planter class was more thoroughly destroyed than the nobility and clergy during the French Revolution. Their total loss in property and slaves is estimated at $5.36 billion (Dubois, 1964 [1934], pp. 128-9, 605).

The important point is that blacks played a major role in the destruction of slavery and thereby helped shape the succeeding class structure. Dudley Cornish's detailed study of black participation in the Civil War indicates that 186,017 served in the Union Army, taking part in over 449 major and minor engagements. They comprised 10 percent of total Union forces. Approximately one-third or 68,178 of these troops lost their lives (1968, pp. 258-71). In fact, black troops 'suffered 35 percent more casualties than any other group' (Foner, 1981, p. 15).

Including soldiers, servants, laborers and spies, close to 400,000 blacks served the Union Army. President Lincoln observed: 'Abandon all the posts now garrisoned by Black men; take two hundred thousand men from our side and put them in the battlefield or cornfield against us, and we would be compelled to abandon the war in three weeks' (Dubois, 1964, p. 100). For their participation, blacks demanded and were promised ownership and access to lands confiscated from rebellious ex-slave owners. But this promise was quickly rescinded by President Johnson once the war ended (Boston, 1982-3, pp. 445-9).

Following the Civil War, the planters attempted to reorganize the economy of the South under a system of forced labor. Legally, 'Black Codes' were enacted. These laws prohibited labor migration, regulated working conditions on the old plantations, established harsh penalties for vagrancy and in some cases prohibited blacks from purchasing land. Their fundamental intent was to shackle the freed slave to the old plantations, abolish labor market competition, consolidate the new system of labor and reestablish the economic supremacy of the defeated slave oligarchy.

By 1867 this counterrevolution was meeting growing resistance from blacks and Northern whites. Finally, the Congress decided to subdue the planters once and for all by installing, with the aid of federal troops, radical Reconstruction governments in the South. In magnitude of importance, this decision compares with the legal abolition of slavery or the abolition of Jim Crow segregation one century later. Although short lived, it had a profound impact upon the economic, political, educational and social fortunes of blacks (Dubois, 1964).

During Reconstruction – considered in Table 2.1 as 1869 to 1901, but in reality it lasted only until 1880 – blacks were elected to federal and state positions in very significant numbers. Likewise, the number of local elected and appointed officials was considerable, but a numerical count is more difficult to obtain.

The greatest number of blacks elected to Congress in any one term was seven, which occurred in 1873-5 and 1875-7. This number was not matched again for almost one hundred years, until the 1967-9 congressional term (US DOC, 1979, p. 148). Further, as a proportion of the population, black congressional representation today still does not match the peak of the Reconstruction period. The 1986 fall elections placed a record twenty-three blacks in the 100th Congress, bringing the total to one for every 1.15 million blacks. At the height of Reconstruction, there was one black congressman for every 800,000 blacks.

Despite the many progressive educational, social-welfare and legal changes instituted during the period, Dubois (1964, esp. ch. XIV) has suggested that Reconstruction was used also for a second purpose: that is, to establish favorable conditions for economic domination of the South by Northern finance and industry. Once accomplished, the federal government withdrew

Table 2.1 Black Elected Officials during Reconstruction, 1869-1901

	Senators	Representatives	Total
Federal legislators	2	20	22
State legislators	124	670	794

Source: US Department of Commerce (DOC), 1979, p. 155.

its troops and allowed a violent counterrevolution to occur. This time, the Ku Klux Klan and similar organizations, operating in the interest of the ex-planters, purged the South of all Reconstruction governments. Voting rights were rescinded and property rights attacked. Blacks were driven legally and forcibly out of local, state and federal political offices. By 1901 there was not a single black elected to a federal office, a situation which remained true for the South until 1971, while in the North the first black congressman was not elected until 1929; and there remained only one until 1947 (US DOC, 1979, pp. 148, 154).

A vicious but legally sanctioned era of Jim Crow segregation was about to begin. Economically the forced labor system gave way to a new stage of black land tenancy. In the South, blacks were relegated to the agricultural sector or to the lowest strata of the non-agricultural occupations. Within agriculture they were overwhelmingly sharecroppers. Of the 2.74 million gainfully employed black workers in the South in 1890, 62 percent were in the agricultural sector, while 28 percent were in domestic and personal services. In the North and West, 63 percent were in domestic and personal services, while 16 percent were in agriculture. Only one-fourth of the 746,717 black farm operators in the South in 1900 were owners; the remainder were tenant farmers. Finally, 60 percent of the tenants were sharecroppers (US Department of Agriculture, 1969, p. 21; US DOC, 1979, pp. 73, 81; Boston, 1982-3, p. 458).

By this time the practice of relegating blacks to the lowest segment of the labor market was well established. Yet this was not always the case. Green and Woodson (1930) and Foner (1981) found blacks in both the South and North to be well represented among the skilled trades during the antebellum period.

> The prominence of the Negro in skilled lines was very evident in the cities of the South. An incomplete list of occupations of free Negroes of Charleston, New Orleans and Louisville of 1859 shows that they were connected with a wide variety of enterprises . . .
> It was inevitable also that the large place which the Negro occupied in the sk:¹led trades would bring them into competition with whites and cause antagonism.
>   (Green and Woodson, 1930, pp. 14, 15)

Beginning in the 1830s, Southern legislatures were petitioned to prohibit blacks from skilled trades. In 1845 Georgia passed an Act prohibiting all blacks, slave or free, from becoming mechanics. Mississippi, Maryland, North Carolina, South Carolina and Virginia followed quickly with similar restrictive legislation (Green and Woodson, 1930, pp. 15-18). After the Civil War, the 'Black Codes' and Jim Crow laws completed the purging of blacks from skilled occupational categories. In the North the outcome was similar, but the process differed. In the early 1800s the successive waves of white immigrants drove blacks out of skilled trades. Frederick Douglas lamented: 'Every hour sees the black man elbowed out of employment by some newly arrived immigrant whose hunger and whose color are thought to give him a better title to the place' (cited in Foner, 1981, p. 6). The dispossession of black artisans and skilled labor in the North also involved violent race riots and the exclusion of blacks from every labor union. Thus a retrogression in the status of free black labor set in. But this is often forgotten when, in recounting labor history, authors depict blacks only as strike breakers in the early union movement.

The black land tenant class consisted of the landowning farmer, the sharecropper, the share tenant and the cash renter. Of the four, sharecroppers were most numerous, since many whites resented black landownership, and most blacks lacked access to cash and credit.

In descending order of social prestige and income, the landowner was followed by the cash renter, the share tenant and, at the bottom, the sharecropper. In certain regions of the South, blacks were relegated exclusively to sharecropping, while share tenancy was considered to be a white institution (Conrad, 1965, p. 7). The sharecropper differed from the share tenant by the means of production he provided and consequently by the extent of participation in the 'split' of the output. The cropper was provided all means of production including land, tools, feed, seed, fertilizer and a house. As a result, the split on paper was usually only fifty-fifty while in practice it was even less: particularly once the 'furnishings' were deducted. The share tenant provided his own feed, seed, tools, stock and fertilizer. His share was usually two-thirds to three-fourths of the output.

By the 1930s the collapse of black land tenancy had set in. The chief causes of the demise were the absence of a material interest on the part of the tenant to increase productivity, the rapid pace of mechanization in cotton production west of the Mississippi relative to the slow pace in the black belt, the low rate of reinvestment by Southern landlords, soil depletion in cotton regions, increasing foreign competition and the Great Depression (Boston 1982-3).

The tenant had also to contend with the boll weevil, the contrivance and exploitation of the landowners[1] and the usury of middle merchants. In fact, an entire folklore developed around the sharecropper's predicament, as best illustrated in this often-repeated anecdote:

> A tenant offering five bales of cotton was told, after some owl-eyed figuring, that this cotton exactly balanced his debt. Delighted at the prospect of a profit this year, the tenant reported that he had one more bale which he hadn't yet brought in. 'Shucks,' shouted the boss, 'why didn't you tell me before? Now I will have to figure the account all over again to make it come out even.'
>
> (Johnson, Embree and Alexander, 1935, p. 9)

Table 2.2 illustrates how rapidly the black land tenant class was driven into extinction, particularly the sharecropper. The political and ideological superstructure of the era was often violent, and the courts, lynching, Klan terror, Jim Crow laws, political disenfranchisement and financial indebtedness were used alternately

Table 2.2 Tenure of Black Farm Operators, 1910-74

| | Black farm operators, South | | | | |
	1910	1940	1959	1969	1974
Owners	229,898	170,070	127,896	68,028	29,512
Tenants	649,176	500,799	138,844	17,220	5,523
Sharecroppers	355,858	383,834	106,536	—	—
Per cent blacks are of all tenants	43.6%	35.0%	36.2%	13.4%	5.9%
Per cent blacks are of all sharecroppers	37.7%	38.1%	42.8%	—	—

Source: US Department of Agriculture, 1974; US DOC, 1979.

to maintain the structures of racial domination and to keep blacks tied to the land.

Faced with these conditions in the South and attracted by war-related demand in the North, the main response of the black tenant was mass out-migration (Campbell and Johnson, 1981). This opened a new stage of development – one leading to an urbanized wage labor force.

As blacks migrated to the North and West their occupational distribution improved. In 1890, 80 percent of blacks lived in rural areas and over 90 percent resided in the South. By 1940 this population was 33 percent non-South and 49 percent urbanized. In 1960 these percentages were 40 percent and 73 percent respectively (US DOC, 1979, p. 14). The changes in black class structures and consciousness accompanying this rapid urbanization and new occupational distribution are captured in Frazier's *Black Bourgeoisie* (1957).

The pressures of urbanization along with the persistence of segregation barriers produced the Civil Rights Movement – which altered once again the internal structure of black social classes. But in the midst of this social, political and ideological upheaval, an unprecedented era of economic stagnation and structural transformation set in. So while the Civil Rights and Black Power movements opened new doors for the development of a new black capitalist class and a new black middle class, stagnation and long-term structural changes in the economy were leading to a progressive marginalization of a growing percentage of black workers. What then has been the impact of these developments on the contemporary structure of black social classes? We turn next to this issue.

The Anatomy of Classes

The preceding section was designed to demonstrate the historical impact of economic, social and political factors on the class stratification of black society. It made clear the central role that racial conflict plays in this process. The remaining sections examine black social classes today, the structure of which is illustrated in Figure 2.2.

There are three main classes, each determined fundamentally by its ownership relation to the means of production. Their internal

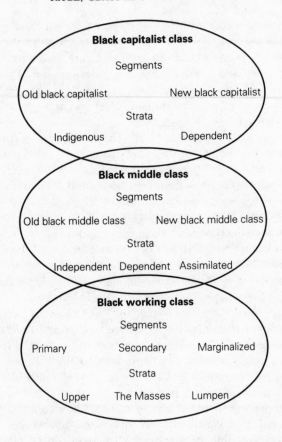

Figure 2.2 Class structure of black society.

structures consist of segments and strata. Segments are composed of individuals having similar life chances derived from common functions in the division of labor and similar patterns of income distribution. Strata consist of individuals with similar ideological and political orientations, that is, common expressions of class consciousness. We contend that there exists a significant correlation between class segments and class strata, but it is far from exact and cannot be deduced in a deterministic manner. This idea is depicted in Figure 1.3 of Chapter 1. Further, strata are not mutually exclusive. They will intersect just as do the boundaries of classes. In Figure 2.2 each stratum is placed beneath the segment with which it has the highest correlation. Again this does not preclude it from having correlations with other segments, but it does mean such relations are weaker or secondary.[2]

The Black Capitalist Class

During the period of slavery and immediately afterwards, the major avenue open to blacks for the accumulation of capital was landownership. By 1860 there were approximately 488,000 free blacks among a total black population of 4.4 million. Prior to emancipation, this free population had accumulated about $50 million in wealth (Harris, 1936, p. 9).

Although landownership was key, with the defeat of Reconstruction blacks were expropriated of both redistributed lands and capital accumulated through years of saving. They were dispossessed also of a political and judicial mechanism to protect property rights. This event constituted the single most devastating blow to the establishment of a viable black capitalist class in America; and even during the decades since, access of black entrepreneurs to capital has been extremely restricted. For example, as recently as 1971 black banks granted $60 million of the $150 million in loans made to black businesses. That year, assets of black-owned banks were only $600 million, or less than one-tenth of one percent of the $700 billion in assets of the nation's white banks. Yet black banks accounted for 33 percent of all loans to black businesses. Only one generation earlier, 86 percent of blacks entering business had to depend exclusively on personal savings (*Black Enterprise*, 1973, p. 51).

Despite its embryonic state, until the Civil Rights Movement, proprietors of banks, savings and loan associations and insurance companies constituted the most well-to-do segment of the black capitalist class. The origin of these enterprises dates to the African benevolent societies, fraternities and mutual relief associations founded at the beginning of the nineteenth century (Foner, 1981, pp. 10, 11; Frazier, 1957, pp. 35-41). It was this urge among blacks to establish thrift associations that led Congress to charter the Freedman's Savings and Trust Company (Freedman's Bank) between 1865 and 1874.

This bank, which was restricted to black depositors but controlled by a congressionally appointed board, recorded over $55 million in deposits of some 44,000 mainly poor black farmers and laborers. As originally chartered, two-thirds of the deposits were to be invested in government securities. Attracted by its rapid growth, however, white speculators persuaded Congress to amend the bank's charter. This allowed the hard-earned savings of ex-slaves to be loaned to risky and unscrupulous investors, and by 1873 the enterprise was bankrupted. Writing in 1880, William Wells Brown, an ex-slave and successful writer, lamented the bank's failure as a major financial and psychological blow to blacks.

> The hope of everyone seemed to center in the Freedman's Savings Bank. 'This is our bank,' said they and to this institution the intelligent and the ignorant, the soldier, farmer, day laborer and poor washerwoman all alike brought their earnings . . . The announcement, therefore, of the closing of the Bank had a paralyzing effect upon blacks everywhere.
> Large numbers quit work; the greater portion sold their bank-books for a trifle. Many who had purchased small farms and had paid part of the purchase money, became discouraged, gave up the lands and went about as if every hope was lost. Verily, the failure of the Freedman's Savings Bank was a national calamity, the influence of which will be felt for many years.
> (Brown, 1976 [1880], pp. 260-1)

The first privately owned black bank, the True Reformer, was organized in 1888. Between that year and 1934, 134 black-owned banks were organized. But mainly, the early black capitalists established service and retail enterprises as opposed to manufacturing establishments. The former were more immune to the vagaries of racial animosity. This early history is reflected still in the character of black enterprises today. Table 2.3 lists receipts of the ten largest industry groups of black-owned firms.

In 1982, of 339,239 black-owned firms, 68.2 percent were concentrated in selected services and retail trade, accounting for 59.2 percent of total gross receipts of $12.4 billion. Firms with paid employees accounted for 11.4 percent of the total number and 68.6 percent of gross receipts. There were only 136 firms with 100 or more employees. They accounted for 16.5 percent of

Table 2.3 The Ten Largest Major Industry Groups in Receipts
of Black-Owned Firms, 1982

SIC code	Industry group	Number of firms	Receipts ($ million)
55	Automotive dealers and service stations	3,448	1,307
59	Miscellaneous retail	53,981	993
54	Food stores	9,187	883
58	Eating and drinking places	11,629	675
80	Health services	17,195	595
17	Special trade contractors	18,399	578
72	Personal services	40,394	561
51	Wholesale trade, non-durable goods	2,441	550
42	Trucking and warehousing	13,029	530
50	Wholesale trade, durable goods	1,210	309

Source: US DOC, 1985, pp. 1, 2.

total receipts. Forty-seven percent of the firms had gross receipts
of less than $5,000 – see Table 2.4(a) and (b).

If we divide the black capitalist class into two segments – an 'old
black capitalist' and a 'new black capitalist' (see Figure 2.2) – the
impact of racism can be seen more clearly. The old segment has
three distinguishing features. First, its enterprises evolved mainly
before the Civil Rights era and were constrained to operating in
an environment of racial segregation. Second, the most significant
implication here is that their clientele was black almost exclusively.
Third, these constraints tied the fortunes of entrepreneurs of this
segment to the economic, political and social developments in
the black community. It is interesting to note that as segregation
diminished so did the exclusive access of these businesses to the
black consumer; and, as a result, many are presently stagnating.
But it should not be concluded that segregation benefited black
business development. The constraints it imposed far outweighed
the advantages of a captive clientele.

Because its products are marketed exclusively to blacks, the old
black capitalist segment has a greater affiliation with and interest
in political, social and economic developments in the community.

Table 2.4(a) Sales and Receipts of Minority-Owned Firms, 1982

Industry division and receipt size	All firms		Firms with paid employees		
	Number of firms	Sales and receipts ($1,000)	Number of firms	Employees for pay period including 12 March	Sales and receipts ($1,000)
All industries	339,239	12,443,572	38,631	165,765	8,529,062
Less than $5,000	158,672	290,541	933	888	2,781
$5,000 to $9,999	53,809	386,450	1,647	1,351	12,570
$10,000 to $24,999	59,192	940,145	6,014	6,070	104,641
$25,000 to $49,999	30,253	1,067,014	8,005	11,838	293,289
$50,000 to $99,999	19,554	1,365,443	8,899	20,549	638,813
$100,000 to $199,999	9,855	1,365,283	6,431	22,940	903,483
$200,000 to $249,999	1,885	420,323	1,440	7,382	321,356
$250,000 to $499,999	3,409	1,165,069	2,826	18,894	970,652
$500,000 to $999,999	1,481	1,019,915	1,341	15,047	926,079
$1,000,000 or more	1,129	4,423,389	1,095	60,806	1,355,398

Table 2.4(b) Employee Size of Minority-Owned Firms, 1982

Industry division and employment size	Number of firms	Employees for pay period including 12 March	Sales and receipts ($1,000)
All industries	339,239	165,765	12,443,572
With no paid employees	300,608	—	3,914,510
With paid employees	38,631	165,765	8,529,062
No employees	6,612	—	291,273
1 to 4 employees	25,027	44,854	2,449,238
5 to 9 employees	4,264	27,259	1,181,951
10 to 19 employees	1,611	21,159	875,620
20 to 49 employees	759	22,660	1,332,128
50 to 99 employees	222	14,912	990,210
100 employees or more	136	34,921	1,408,642

Source: US DOC, 1985, pp. 90, 92.

Also, while its restricted economic base slowed its rate of capital accumulation, it provided these entrepreneurs greater political autonomy from whites in advocating social reforms. For this reason, we classify such entrepreneurs as part of the indigenous stratum of the black capitalist class.

There is a loose analogy here between this stratum and the 'national bourgeoisie' in Third World countries. Because the latter's economic operations are domestically financed and organized, it is perceived to have political interests that are linked closely to indigenous development. This contrasts with the *'comprador bourgeoisie'*, or the segment of the capitalist class in a Third World country whose economic operations are organized and financed by multinational corporations of advanced industrial countries. Its foreign economic links are perceived to bind the local *comprador* ideologically and politically to the foreign interest instead of the national interest (Poulantzas, 1973, p. 39).

The New Black Capitalist

The new black capitalist segment contrasts sharply with the old. Its development dates primarily to the transition period of

35

the late 1960s and early 1970s. For example, sixty-four of the 1983 *Black Enterprise* 100 largest corporations were founded since 1970 (*Black Enterprise*, 1983, p. 72). These new enterprises have transcended the boundaries imposed upon the old black capitalist segment and depend to a greater extent on a white clientele, the general corporate sector and subcontracts from the government. For example, in 1982 small minority-owned businesses received $2.6 billion in federal government prime contract awards (US Small Business Administration [SBA], 1984, p. 384). As a result of their more diverse clientele, the economic fortunes of such enterprises are not tied as closely to the black community. This causes their ideological and political affiliation with the community to be weaker.

In a detailed study of the growth dynamics of minority enterprises, Bates observes:

> Since the 1960s, the traditionally backward minority business community has begun to diversify and expand in response to an influx of talent and capital. Aggregate figures on all minority-owned businesses understate this progress because they fail to identify two divergent trends: 1) absolute decline among many traditional lines of business, and 2) progress in nontraditional emerging fields.
>
> (1986, p. 1)

Well-educated black entrepreneurs have been attracted in increasing numbers to finance, insurance, real estate, business services, manufacturing, wholesale and professional services. On the other hand, personal service as a category of black-owned business is rapidly declining, both in percent of entrepreneurs and in returns to self-employment (Bates, 1986, p. 2).

The social consciousness of this new black capitalist segment differs from that of the old black capitalist because its economic base is more external. As such, its identification and affiliation with the black community are weaker because it is more dependent upon whites economically. Still, the extremely small size of the black capitalist class makes it difficult to distinguish its political consciousness with real precision, and these perceptions are derived mainly from participatory observations. But we have taken care to structure each hypothesis in a testable fashion.

Despite the external economic ties of this new black capitalist segment we note that its political and social outlook and interests are still connected, albeit in a looser fashion, to the black community. This is because its existence and success are due largely to civil rights agitation.

The Civil Rights era, of which the Black Power Movement was an integral part, created the conditions for an alteration in the internal structure of the black capitalist class and the growth of a new black capitalist segment. In an attitudinal study of sixty New York businessmen, Boneparth (1976, p. 30) found the following responses to be typical:

> When you ask about the black militant, I have to say I appreciate the changes he helped bring out in the last ten years. Unless there were people running around the streets throwing bricks, I wouldn't be where I am. It wasn't until the riots that we got legislation in the Johnson administration.
>
> It took a Rap Brown and a Stokely to make [white] business look around and talk to Whitney Young. If they weren't burning down cities and having riots, the business environment wouldn't have asked 'who can we talk to?'

The assault on segregation allowed more black businesses and entrepreneurs to break out of their isolation and gain increased access to capital, knowledge, experience and markets earlier denied them. This injected dynamism into newly established black capitalist enterprises.

Three factors affect the entry, survival, growth and profitability of black businesses and business in general: first, sufficient and appropriate education; second, relevant occupational training; and third, adequate individual or family income or access to other forms of capital and credit (US SBA, 1984, p. 371). Diminishing segregation barriers in education and industry have allowed blacks to acquire these prerequisites in greater numbers.

Between 1977 and 1980 black-owned businesses increased by 47 percent (US DOC, 1985). But more significantly, in 1960 personal services and retail accounted for the largest percentage of self-employed minority workers, representing 29 percent and 25 percent respectively. By 1980 these accounted for 13 percent and 22 percent respectively where nontraditional categories increased from 10 percent to 19 percent (US SBA, 1984, pp. 83, 84). The editors of *Black Enterprise* have observed that this growing business strength reflects

> the increasingly strong desire of all black business owners to compete in a greater variety of industries, to pay more sophisticated attention to the black consumer market, and to expand their clientele beyond the black market.
>
> (1983, p. 68)

We cite these trends for two reasons. First, they are completely ignored when the black capitalist class is merged with the black middle class as is commonly done in class analyses. But second and most importantly, they illustrate that, freed from the fetters of racial inequality, the black entrepreneur displays the same capacities as other US ethnic groups. Although a seemingly trivial observation, it is worth noting because cross-cultural comparisons of ethnic minorities conducted by conservatives often leave the impression that black economic inequality is due in part to the absence of the spirit of enterprise that exists among other more successful ethnic groups. Yet one need not make such comparisons to determine the relative impact of discrimination on black attainment. Instead, we only have to consider the accelerated advance of the new black capitalist segment, which has been impacted less by the strictures of racial inequality.

Although more successful, the rapid growth of this new segment is still not significant enough to alter the status of the entire black capitalist class. By whatever measure one chooses, whether number of employees, size of gross revenues, asset ownership, or some other criterion, the black capitalist class is minuscule. Given its present state, is it correct to maintain that race is not a factor in its development? Even if all discriminatory practices have ceased, and they certainly have not, the current structure of the black capitalist class is the product of a history of racial subordination which has left it extremely unequal in every meaningful respect. Furthermore, it is unlikely that such an enormous gap can be closed in the foreseeable future.

The small size of the black capitalist class has meant two things. First, it exerts little influence over major developments within the black community, and has produced historically almost no popular or mass leaders. Second, it would be incorrect to view it as a major agent of internal class conflict.

The Black Middle Class

The black middle class may be subdivided into two segments: the old and the new. While the origin of the former predates the Civil War, the latter is a consequence of the changing structure of the economy and the new opportunities opened by the Civil Rights era. The old black middle class segment is distinguishable by the way it earns its means of livelihood: living mainly off its own effort through the ownership and operation of small businesses or services. In this category are self-employed people such as doctors, lawyers, shopowners, barbers, beauticians, funeral directors and carpenters.

As indicated earlier, there has recently been an expansion of the new black middle class. This segment consists of individuals endowed with scarce forms of knowledge, skills and laboring abilities. These skills are acquired usually through advanced education, training, or specialized apprenticeships. Individuals possessing these abilities include scientists, engineers, professors, technicians, professional athletes and entertainers. Where the old middle class is self-employed, these individuals are not, but instead sell their labor to business and industry at unusually high salaries, and the relative scarcity of their skills permits this market power. These salaries distinguish this segment from ordinary workers, who also sell their labor.[3]

Just as segregation forced most black businessmen of the old capitalist class to operate in a restricted market, it did likewise to small businesses of the old black middle class. In 1972 the author conducted a survey of businesses in the Hogan's Creek district of Jacksonville, Florida. This area, immediately adjacent to downtown, once constituted the center of black socioeconomic life. Even in 1972 the neighborhood still had the highest concentration of black-owned businesses but was in rapid decline due primarily to suburbanization and urban renewal. Of the 135 business establishments, the 73 black-owned ones were distributed as follows: personal service (14); confectionery (13); retail (11); restaurant

(10); repair (5); entertainment and recreation (5); funeral home (4); professional service (4); drug, apparel and grocery stores (2 each); insurance (1).

The average number of employees per firm was 2.7. With the exception of insurance companies, professional service and funeral homes, most black-owned firms earned less than $10,000 of net income per year. The distribution by net income for all firms responding to the survey was as follows: 42 earned less than $5,000, 28 earned between $5,000 and $10,000, and 30 earned greater than $10,000 (Boston, 1972). At the time, Jacksonville's population of 622,000 was one-fourth black. Yet there was a total of only 984 black firms, employing only 1,111 people, 400 of whom were employed by one firm – the Afro-American Life Insurance Company. The average net receipts were $6,000; gross receipts were $26,408 (US DOC, 1971). This distorted development of Jacksonville's old black middle class is not atypical and brings into clearer focus the impact of segregation.

Osborne and Granfield (1976, p. 530, citing Bates, 1973) indicate that during the segregation era businessmen had limited access to capital markets and limited educational opportunities. As a result, they survived by restricting their activities to small-scale enterprises requiring minimal capital outlays. Coleman and Cook assert:

> It is not unreasonable to assume that during the nineteenth century and until the 1960s, prospective black businessmen were rather reluctant to start a business beyond the 'mom and pop' variety. For indeed, any large scale enterprise would have been in all probability dependent in some way upon white suppliers and/or white consumers either or both of which would have probably proved hostile. Furthermore, black entrepreneurs faced the very real possibilities of receiving either physical harm or destruction of their property by antagonistic white competitors or bigots.
>
> (1976, p. 46)

Because of the small size of most black businesses one might object to placing them in the middle class. But such distorted developments in the black class structure are precisely what we are attempting to illustrate. The 'mom and pop' nature of small black businesses cannot be understood in isolation from the historical barriers of racial inequality; and excluding such businesses from the black middle class because their income is low omits the very question that needs answering.

Ironically, during the segregation era the economic weakness of the black middle and capitalist classes caused class consciousness and identification to center on factors such as skin color, club or fraternity membership, social standing vis-a-vis white society, family background and a variety of noneconomic circumstances. In *Black Bourgeoisie* (1957), Frazier describes these distorted forms of consciousness; and blacks old enough to have lived during this period can attest that such factors stratified black society perhaps even more sharply than differential wealth ownership does today.

Many leaders of black society have come from the old black middle class. Their occupations have included clergymen, doctors, lawyers, educators and small independent businessmen. In a detailed study of the black power structure of a Providence, Rhode Island, community, Pfautz (1962, p. 161) conducted a poll to determine the top leaders, ranked from one to sixteen. The results were as follows: agency director, mortician, maintenance superintendent, management analyst, agency director, real-estate agent, lawyer, union official, post office clerk, physician, lawyer, minister, bank manager, trucker, mortician and housewife. Noticeably represented are middle- and working-class occupations.

The New Black Middle Class

The Civil Rights era propelled significant numbers into the new black middle class. The distinguishing feature of this segment is its possession of scarce skills and the very high wages and salaries this engenders. Blacks employed as corporate executives, managers, technicians, scientists, engineers, specialists, academicians and so on are part of this new class segment.

Table 2.5 is a very crude approximation of the sizes of the black and white middle classes. It is an approximation for several reasons. First of all, it is extremely difficult to give a precise numerical figure to the size of a social class, and every attempt to do so will only engender other factors that have not been considered. For this reason, we do not pursue this issue beyond what is given

Table 2.5 The Black Middle Class, 1982, an Approximation

Occupation and class fraction	Total black	Total nonblack
Old middle class	80,984	3,235,012
Self-employed retail	27,650	810,346
Self-employed except retail and farm	35,910	990,090
Farmers and farm managers	17,424	1,434,576
New middle class	1,288,861	23,714,139
Managerial, technical and professional †		
Health	238,199	3,024,801
Professional and technical	552,366	9,869,634
Managers and administrators	385,200	9,244,800
Blue-collar supervisors	113,096	1,574,904
Total middle class	1,369,845	26,949,151
Percent of employed workers	14.96%	29.82%

† This category includes non-self-employed engineers, physicians, registered nurses, post-secondary teachers, lawyers, judges, etc.

Source: US Department of Labor (DOL), 1983, pp. 179,154.

in Table 2.5. Using our crude technique, the black middle class numbers over 1.3 million and constitutes about 15 percent of the black employed population. On the other hand, the white middle class constitutes 29.8 percent of its employed population. If these calculations are made as a percent of the civilian labor force, the black middle class decreases to only 11 percent while the white middle class constitutes 27 percent. The differential is due to the greater unemployment experienced by blacks and is only one of several complications encountered when measuring the size of classes by occupational distribution.

Using an income threshold, arbitrarily chosen, some studies estimate the black middle class at 40 percent of the black population

– a figure which seems by intuition much too high (see Pinkney, 1984, p. 102 for a critique of these).

Another often neglected problem is classifying the entire family when the occupations of husbands and wives are very different. For example, if one spouse is a physician and the other a clerk, we typically think of the family as part of the middle class and not the working class. This is because the household head having the most prestigious production relation generally has the greatest influence on the social status of the family.

We run into difficulty using occupations to identify the middle class. But income thresholds produce even worse results. Suppose a self-employed professional receives little or no net income during the survey year. Despite an otherwise stable location within the middle class, this person will be classified as part of a lower class. On the other hand, suppose an ordinary laborer receives a large but transitory increase in income during the survey year. The individual would be classified as part of a higher class, when by all other standards he belongs to the working class. By establishing such arbitrary income boundaries one cannot make judgements on the stability of class relation examined.

This instability is not a trivial issue. For example, using the Social Security Administration's Continuous Work History Sample data to trace longitudinally the income change of 158,439 workers between 1973 and 1975, we found that 25.1 percent experienced absolute income losses, the mean of which was $2,997. On the other hand, between 1973-5, 45.5 percent of individuals examined experienced real income gains, the mean of which was $4,535 (Boston, 1987a). Some authors conducting class analyses have acknowledged the instability of income. Unfortunately such recognition has not prompted a challenge to the practice of basing class definitions on income criteria.

Origin of Black Conservatism

To understand the origin of black neoconservative ideology we must investigate strata of the black middle class. The independent stratum stands at the political and ideological left of its class. It is made up overwhelmingly of members from the old segment of the black middle class (BMC), whose occupations and means of livelihood tie them closely to the black community. Charles Johnson's important sociological study (1970 [1943]) captures the essence of black businessmen within this stratum.

> In this class are many of the self-conscious negroes who patronize negro businesses as a matter of race loyalty and condemn other negroes, upper and lower, for not doing the same. A negro man of this class commented . . . 'I believe in my race and do everything I can to help any of them along. I never buy anything from a white man I can get from a colored man. Everybody don't do it, though . . . Professor [. . .] across the street, he gets his (newspaper) from a white boy. He's making his living off the colored people and gives the white boys his money.'
>
> (Johnson, 1970, p. 233)

Because of this stratum's economic foundation it identifies closely with popular political movements within the black community – and the latter are very liberal or even radical on occasions.

Since we are familiar with the ideology and activities of political activists and their associated organizations, we use them to illustrate our point. Many popular black activists and organizations have belonged to this 'independent' stratum. Historical figures include W. E. B. Dubois and Paul Robeson. More contemporary figures are Jesse Jackson of the Rainbow Coalition and Louis Farrakan of the Nation of Islam. Again, this stratum's close economic and social ties to black society orient its consciousness towards 'grass-roots' black opinion, which is, for historical reasons, most often very liberal or even radical at times.

At the center of the political and ideological spectrum is the 'dependent BMC'. Its members are drawn simultaneously from the old and the new black middle-class fractions. In most cases they have close social, organizational, cultural and political connections to black society. But their economic means of livelihood are derived in part or in total from white society. Classic examples of this dependent stratum are the historically black colleges, traditional civil rights organizations, black consulting and public relations firms, black politicians and others working for the government, major corporations and predominantly white colleges and universities.

This stratum's close social connection to black society, but alongside its economic dependence upon sources external to that society, most often places it in an intermediate or vacillating position vis-a-vis grass-roots black political activity. While its members will always support nonviolent social change and electoral politics, seldom will they support more radical movements. It is torn between identifying with the needs and demands of the black masses, with whom it has close social connections, and having to pacify the anxieties of white society, which provides its means of economic livelihood.

Nonviolence is usually a buzzword to identify this stratum, and its foremost representatives were leaders such as Booker T. Washington, Whitney Young and Martin Luther King, during his latter years. Today's representatives of this stratum include most of the prominent black elected officials as well as the civil rights organizations and their leadership.

There has always been a tug of war for leadership over black society between the dependent BMC and independent BMC strata. This was epitomized by the debate between Booker T. Washington and W. E. B. Dubois at the turn of the century. During the Civil Rights era such conflict existed between the established leadership of the NAACP, the SCLC, the Urban League and leaders of the Black Power Movement. Most recently Jesse Jackson's presidential campaign sparked a similar conflict between Jackson and many nationally prominent black politicians and civil right leaders who continued to support the traditional Democratic Party machinery. We believe the ideological positions expressed in these polemics generally reflect the differences in class position of the participants. Still, it is not our intention to be rigid about this general observation.

Our position is that there exists a significant correlation between black class strata and class segments. We cannot attach a numerical value to the strength of the relation because it is derived from participatory observation rather than empirical investigation. We also do not mean to imply that everyone in the same economic position expresses a similar ideological outlook.

With the growing ascendancy of the new black middle class, a third ideological trend has developed and is represented by an assimilated stratum of the BMC. The distinguishing feature of this stratum is a social, cultural, political and organizational alienation from mainstream black society and black public opinion. Politically, this alienation forces it to the far right of the black middle class and black society in general and has given rise to the new black conservatism. Today many of its foremost spokesmen work for either the government, major white universities, or foundations and are closely affiliated with the conservative political tide sweeping mainstream politics in America. Because of this alliance, the stratum's ideologues currently enjoy a notoriety far out of proportion to their actual influence within black society. The characteristics of their economic philosophy have already been described in the opening sections of Chapter 1. In Chapter 3 we will assess fully the theoretical validity of these propositions, which are most clearly expressed in the writings of Thomas Sowell (1981, 1984) and Walter Williams (1982b).

A conservative stratum has always existed within the black class structure, but we are presently experiencing its most significant attempt to exert ideological influence over black society. As expected, this influence grows and dwindles with the political fortunes of mainstream conservatism. This is because there exists no independent organizational, ideological, or economic base of conservatism within the black community of any significance. Although currently small, as the new black middle class expands in size this stratum can be expected to grow and pose an increasing challenge to the independent and dependent middle-class strata. But this still depends upon the extent to which the general conservative movement wields influence. Fundamentally, its alienation from 'the masses' will cause its influence upon black society to always be extremely limited.

The Black Worker

The working class, as defined in Chapter 1, is distinguished by the way it earns its means of livelihood. Specifically, it must sell its laboring abilities to employers. This class consists of three segments: a primary segment, a secondary segment and a marginalized segment. These correspond respectively to three strata: the upper stratum, the masses and the lumpen stratum.

Presently, there are many attempts to define or redefine the working class. Some authors exclude from it all white-collar workers and place them in the new middle class. For others, the major disagreement centers on the definition of productive and nonproductive workers – where productive workers, considered to be only those in manufacturing occupations, are included in the working class. Others agree with this approach but disagree on the definition of productive workers.

There seems to be little relevance in defining the working class by productive and nonproductive labor, even if the latter were more clearly defined. This is because it would be very hard if not impossible to correlate forms of social consciousness with manufacturing or nonmanufacturing labor, or some similar criterion. In fact, such an approach would be overly deterministic.

Much of the controversy on the definition of the working class can be resolved if a distinction is made between the boundary of the class and the internal segments of the class. In Chapter 1 we provided a definition of the working class which is based upon the approach outlined by Marx (1967). There workers are considered to be individuals who must labor under the control of others to earn their means of livelihood because they do not own or control the means of production. This characteristic constitutes the criterion used to establish the boundary of the class. In order to delineate its internal segments we draw heavily upon the labor market-segmentation literature developed over the last two decades (Doeringer and Piore, 1971; Harrison, 1972; Piore, 1969). This theory and approach is fully elaborated in Chapter 4. Briefly, the approach maintains that there is a dichotomy in the way workers are related to the production process. Some base this dichotomy, which consists of an upper and a lower segment of the labor market, on industry characteristics, while others base it on occupation, race, or even gender. Whatever criterion is used, the theory maintains that enhancement of one's labor ability, through education, training, or the acquisition of additional experience, is insufficient to promote upward mobility from the lower segment of the work force to the upper segment.

Segmented labor markets exhibit a dual character. At one pole are primary jobs and industries. Firms in such industries possess significant monopoly power, high labor productivity and above-average profitability. Primary workers experience more stable

47

employment, relatively higher wages, better working conditions and more advancement opportunities. By contrast, the secondary sector is characterized by more labor-intensive, low-prestige occupations and industries that generally face intense competition and have less stable product demand. The unskilled labor demanded by this sector is paid lower wages. According to the theory, working conditions are such that higher labor turnover and job instability are more typical (Harrison and Sum, 1979).

Racial discrimination is considered a major factor in the production and reproduction of segmented labor markets. Bergman has stated that classes of jobs are reserved for different castes of workers – men or women, black or white – even when the different castes are 'technically substitutable' in production. Hence, workers must compete within their existing castes (Harrison and Sum, 1979, p. 694, citing Bergman, 1971).

Our conception draws upon the theory as a building block but differs in several respects. First, we define segments strictly by occupational categories as opposed to a mixture of industry, occupation and other economic or social characteristics. Secondly, we offer a precise criterion for segmenting the labor market which is based upon a concept of general and specific labor. Thirdly, we relate segments of the labor market to the internal structure of the working class. Finally, several major conclusions of segmentation theory are rejected (see Chapter 4).

Historically, discrimination was a powerful force in regimenting a disproportionate number of blacks to the secondary sector. Today this segmentation continues even though more overt forms of racism have subsided. In fact, current debate focuses on the contemporary mechanisms of racial inequality given the absence of *de jure* discrimination.

Marginalization

Marginalized workers constitute the third segment of the black working class. By marginalized we mean an involuntary situation where an individual does not have a full-time attachment to a job. For simplicity we limit our definition to the sum of unemployed workers, involuntary part-time workers and discouraged workers.

Yet this category can be expanded to include the welfare and poverty populations. Marginalized workers are eligible to become active full-time laborers. But for economic reasons they are not. Figure 2.3 traces the marginalization of black and white workers as a percent of their potential labor forces over time.

The percent marginalized is calculated by taking the total of involuntary part-time workers, unemployed workers and discouraged workers and dividing by the total civilian labor force plus discouraged workers. The denominator gives one the total potential labor force, while the numerator is the number of marginalized workers. The overall percent for blacks has been twice that of whites, and the former's higher base makes the problem particularly acute. In 1970 the percentages for white and black respectively were 7.7 percent and 15.3 percent. In 1982 these percentages were 14.6 percent and 27 percent respectively.

Marginalization is a dynamic process related to business cycle behavior, growing automation of industry, the export of jobs abroad, relocation of industry, the declining industrial base and a host of other factors. But equally important, the adverse impacts

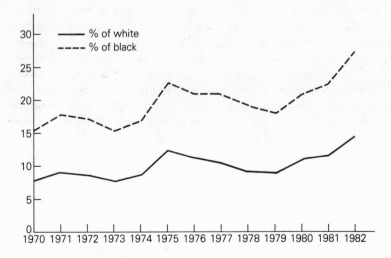

Figure 2.3 Marginalization of black and white workers, 1970–82

Source: US DOL, 1982, 1983, 1985.

of these purely economic forces upon black workers are reinforced by racial inequality. While each factor operates according to its own particular logic, the combined effect has been progressively to reduce the demand for black labor relative to the size of the potential black labor force.

Marginalized workers are surplus laborers, created by economic dynamics in the secondary and primary sectors. Such labor surpluses are usually beneficial to employers, because they make possible an easier substitution of low-wage for high-wage workers, a stricter enforcement of work discipline, increased job competition and a constantly available pool of potential workers to meet the changing conditions of the business cycle. Rosenberg argues:

> the secondary sector should be seen as a reserve labor force for the primary market. In time of economic expansion some secondary workers get pulled up into primary jobs. When a down-swing occurs, many of these people return to the secondary labor market.
>
> (1977, p. 228)

Harrison and Sum believe that admission into the primary sector is so restricted by specific skills, school credentials, race and sex, that labor shortages within this sector are only partially relieved by upward mobility of secondary workers. Instead, 'primary firms may respond to such shortages by importing skilled workers from outside the local economy' (1979, p. 694). Whatever the case, we will demonstrate in Chapter 4 that blacks are disproportionately represented among the secondary sector, that their position within this sector is reproduced constantly and that race plays a major role in this process (Gordon, Edwards and Reich, 1982).

Opposition of Classes

There are three strata of the black working class: the upper stratum, the masses and the lumpen stratum. The latter consists of individuals totally disenfranchised economically and others who earn their livelihood in illegal ways. Members of the upper working stratum are located mainly in the primary sector and to a lesser extent in the secondary sector. Their job stability, greater income and more prestigious occupations allow them a much better lifestyle than the ordinary working class, and this fact is reflected in their political consciousness. While they generally support popular political struggles, such support is usually channeled through established institutions such as churches, civil rights organizations, civic and community organizations. Individuals of this stratum believe very strongly in the 'American Dream' and see racism as the only impediment to achieving it. As a result, they are quite outspoken against discrimination. Generally, they exhibit greater family stability, higher educational attainment and a much higher standard of living.

Typical occupations held by individuals in this stratum are secondary teachers, low-level managers or supervisors, health technicians, mechanics, construction workers, sales-related occupations and certain production workers. Some individuals within these same occupations have political outlooks that are characteristic of 'the masses.' But in most cases the consciousness expressed by 'the masses' is a reflection of their economic location in the secondary and marginalized segments.

The masses, the most liberal and left-leaning stratum of black society, have been the foundation of all great social change experienced by blacks. Occupationally their members are usually secondary-sector or marginalized workers – laborers, food service workers, housekeepers, nursing aids and orderlies, janitors, construction laborers, stock handlers, drivers, retail sales clerks and the like. To borrow a phrase from Malcolm X, these are the 'Field Negroes.'

The consciousness of the masses can be seen more clearly if one reflects upon the debate that emerged during the Civil Rights era on the issue of nonviolence. In the late 1950s and early 1960s civil rights struggles were led nationally by individuals of the dependent black middle class. As expected, this leadership made nonviolence a universal principle, to be practiced at all times and under any circumstance. But by the mid-1960s a formidable challenge emerged to this leadership. It originated among 'the masses' and was reflected in a more radical demand for self-defense. Ideologically, the new trend centered on Malcolm X, and to a lesser extent Robert Williams, and found expression in the slogan 'By Any Means Necessary.'[4]

Organizations such as SNCC (Student Nonviolent Coordinating Committee) quickly adopted and popularized this slogan. In 1963 violent rebellions erupted in Jacksonville, Florida, and Philadelphia, Pennsylvania. These escalated during each succeeding summer, and Lieske (1978) identified a total of 334 which occurred between 1967 and 1969 in 119 different cities. The August 1965 Watts (Los Angeles) rebellion alone is estimated to have had 31,000 directly involved and 72,000 'close spectators.' More than 4,000 were arrested, thousands received personal injuries, and thirty-four were killed (Sears and McConahay, 1973, pp. 9–13).

This issue of violence polarized black leadership, and the dependent black middle class denounced constantly the masses and their leaders for advocating self-defense. In turn, the latter labeled middle-class leaders 'Uncle Toms' and 'House Negroes' and referred to themselves as 'the Masses' and 'the Grass Roots.' These terms were symptomatic of a deepening class conflict in black society (see Malcolm X, 1965, pp. 3–22). In fact, this debate was one of the clearest expressions of internal class divisions within black society in the last quarter-century.

Conclusions

The intention in the first two chapters has been to demonstrate that: (1) significant changes have occurred within the black class structure since the Civil Rights Movement, but contemporary class analyses have failed to grasp correctly the structure of these changes; (2) without an appropriate delineation of classes, one cannot accurately assess the relative importance of class or race on black opportunity; and (3) racial conflict has produced a contemporary black class structure that is quite different and unequal to that of whites. The most obvious differences are: the absence of a viable black bourgeoisie, the relatively small size of the new black middle class and the disproportionate number of marginalized black workers. Subsequent chapters will measure empirically the importance of these factors in comprehending the nature of race relations in the United States.

Notes Chapter 2

1 In 1935 under the Agricultural Adjustment Act's 'plow-up' program, blacks received only $500,000 of $111,405,244 distributed
   (Johnson, Embree, and Alexander, 1935, p. 32).
2 Note that the dependent stratum of the black middle class consists
   of individuals from both the old and new segments of the black
   middle class.
3 By defining class segments in this manner, we have departed
   from the original criterion of distinguishing class boundaries by
   one's ownership relation to the means of production. Instead, this
   is a distribution relation. Although contradictory to our earlier
   approach, it still seems more reasonable than attempts to define
   the new middle class by white-collar jobs, or productive versus
   nonproductive labor.
4 See *Malcolm X Speaks* (1965), and Robert Williams, *Negroes with
   Guns* (1962).

3 Conservative Gospel according to Sowell, Williams and Gilder: Everything but Discrimination

The Conservative Premise

Thomas Sowell has said: 'demagoguery flourishes where something can be said in a few catchy words that would take volumes to disprove' (1984, p. 106). Although intended as a criticism of liberal economists, one can hardly conceive of a more fitting characterization of conservative approaches to racial discrimination. It seems reasonable to assert that income differences between blacks and whites can be accounted for in part by differences in job-related attributes, demographic characteristics and other relevant characteristics. In fact, all major studies of race have attempted to control for these variables and in so doing find that racial discrimination in income still remains. Nonetheless, conservatives contend the latter has all but vanished and attribute what remains to *everything but discrimination*. This conclusion is based on nine central propositions which are presented and investigated in this and subsequent chapters. In earlier chapters we examined and refuted the view that inequality among ethnic groups can be explained by differences in class stratification among the groups. Instead, we demonstrated that differences in class station between blacks and whites are largely a function of racial inequalities. In this chapter we continue our critique by focusing on conservative proportions relating specifically to racial income inequality. These propositions are synthesized from several major conservative treatises on race relations.

Conservative Propositions

Proposition 1: Conservatives contend that the racial difference in earnings between blacks and whites is not a function of discrimination but reflects the inability of researchers to control adequately for age, geographic location, family size and composition, occupational distribution, educational attainment, job experience and other forms of human capital and demographic differences between blacks and whites. Upon controlling for these, they assert, racial income inequality almost disappears. More specifically, the ten- to twenty-year age difference between groups at opposite ends of the income distribution scale causes a large disparity in experience, occupational attainment and income, and partially explains why ethnic groups such as Jewish Americans have higher incomes than blacks.

Conservatives believe also that educational attainment has a similar impact upon income disparities. Younger blacks have attained educational levels comparable to whites and narrowed the aggregate income gap to such an extent that remaining inequality is attributable exclusively to the insufficient education of older blacks. Geographic differences among ethnic groups also explain income disparities. In fact, such differences are more important than racial differences according to Block and Walker (1982, p. 17). In this respect, the heavy concentration of blacks in the South causes black earnings relative to whites to be much lower. Hence, what appears to be income discrimination, conservatives maintain, is only the logical consequence of location preferences. These factors lead them to conclude that discrimination explains very little of the income disparity between blacks and whites.

Proposition 2: Conservatives claim that the cost of discrimination is the wage premium paid to white workers. But competitive markets for labor will not allow the maintenance of such premiums. Exploiting this situation by hiring black workers, a nondiscriminating firm can increase its profits and drive into bankruptcy the discriminating firm. At the same time the net result of this is to eliminate racial discrimination from labor markets – even if this is not the intended objective. Hence, it is theoretically inconceivable and practically impossible to have racial wage differences in a competitive market without such differences reflecting actual differences in individual job-related attributes.

Proposition 3: Firms do not make systematic errors over the long run in hiring laborers. If employers believe that blacks have lower productivities and such perceptions are based on racial prejudices, leading to the unjustified selection of whites over blacks, these practices will not persist unless the perceptions are valid. Otherwise firms having more accurate information will exploit their competitors' ignorance. So racial hiring preferences cannot reflect long-run perceptual discrimination but rather reflect actual human capital differences.

Proposition 4: Ethnic groups having the same color as blacks but different cultures have succeeded in ways that blacks have not. Color therefore cannot be the basis of differential successes in society. Sowell attempts to separate the effect of culture on income from those of race on income by considering the comparative success of West Indians living in the USA, who have a different cultural background but are similar in skin color.

Proposition 5: Some ethnic groups have experienced more oppression than blacks and have advanced much further. This implies that racial oppression cannot be the limiting factor in economic and social development. To establish this point, an examination of ethnic minorities throughout the world is undertaken, the purpose of which is to demonstrate that minorities confronted with discrimination can rise economically. The conservatives' most preferred group in this regard is the Chinese minority in Asian countries.

Proposition 6: Without discrimination, racial groups would still not be alike in their income, wealth, job selection, or any other economic or sociological attribute. This means that numerical inequality or underrepresentation does not provide evidence of discrimination.

Proposition 7: Several factors, commonly perceived as beneficial to blacks, are actually detrimental to their advancement; examples are government regulations, affirmative action, minimum wages and other actions that retard market forces. In criticizing government interference Williams asserts that the major difference

56

between blacks and other ethnic groups is that blacks became urbanized much later or after business and occupational regulations were imposed. This closed off traditional avenues for 'upward mobility' (1982b, p. xvi). Further, despite the good intentions of bureaucrats, affirmative action does more harm than good and benefits only a very small percentage of blacks and the bureaucracy which administers it. Conservatives maintain that this program harms highly competent minority people by making it appear their accomplishments are not due to their own efforts. It also harms unqualified minority people by placing them in positions which 'expose their incompetence'. Finally, they argue against affirmative action because it increases the frustration and lowers the motivation of people excluded and exacerbates racial animosity (Block and Walker, 1982, p. xviii).

Proposition 8: Because the battle for civil rights was fought and won 'two decades ago' and blacks are still behind, the denial of civil rights cannot be viewed as the 'universal explanation of social or racial problems' (Sowell, 1984, p. 139). Further, Sowell maintains, one danger of the present course of civil rights activity is the undermining of minority self-confidence by constantly relying on 'discrimination' and 'hypocritical standards' as a crutch. Equally important, ethnic groups having the least involvement in political activity have made the greatest economic progress. This means that civil rights agitation and affirmative action lead to the opposite of their intended objectives, because both have made it difficult to dismiss incompetent minorities. Therefore, employers are less willing to chance hiring them in the first place.

Proposition 9: Class differences are often misperceived as racial discrimination. Much black inequality can be explained by the greater concentration of blacks among the lower class and the deficiencies in culture generated thereby. Gilder is rather explicit in asserting that racism has nothing to do with the need to maintain a culture of upward mobility.

> If a capitalist system is to expand, it must give social and educational rewards and reinforcements to 'middle-class' discipline and morality. This means that successful families must take care in choosing their associates and those of their children. This process helps the poor by creating a distinctive culture of upward mobility which they may emulate, and it helps the rich

by transmitting upper-class disciplines to their children. The breakdown of these disciplines hurts all classes.

(1981, p. 92)

Methodological Pitfalls

These propositions are common among conservatives as explanations for racial income inequality. Although largely unverified by empirical evidence, they are nonetheless popular. Why is this so? Mainly because conservative polemicists have mastered the art of building mountains of illusions out of molehills of truth. To be sure, there are grains of truth within some of these propositions. But ten percent accuracy is still ninety percent error, and what troubles critics most is the absence of empirical studies in support of these catchy propositions. To what extent empirically is inequality attributable to discrimination as opposed to other personal and demographic attributes? To this question conservatives have provided sweeping conclusions – but conclusions based on anecdotal evidence and hypothetical arguments. Additionally, this manner of argument has allowed them to keep open an escape hatch.

Accused of denying the existence of discrimination, conservatives quickly respond otherwise. Usually by way of a one-sentence disclaimer at the end of a long treatise, they reject having denied the existence of discrimination. Instead, they maintain that their argument is simply that discrimination is 'less real than apparent.' This however is also true of most social phenomena, and such vague assertions cannot constitute the basis of scientific inquiry.

Disclaimers to the contrary, the logical conclusion of conservative arguments is the denial of racial discrimination. Unfortunately they do not do so in a way that allows critics to easily construct empirically testable hypotheses.

The form of discrimination conservatives choose to focus on is also problematic. The various forms of labor market discrimination are well known. First, suppose two individuals or groups differ racially but possess identical job-related characteristics. Then discrimination is present if (other things remaining constant) group B receives a smaller remuneration for its endowment of job characteristics and productivity than does group A – where the criterion for the differential is race. The second type has to do with differential and unequal access to employment. In this case group B possesses similar attributes to A but is more likely to be unemployed simply because of its race; other things are again held constant. Finally, discrimination exists if the job offers made to A are superior to those of B, and in addition the former experiences greater on-the-job mobility because of its race.

Simply stated, labor market discrimination may manifest itself as unjustified differentials in wages (type one), employment (type two) and job status and mobility (type three). In the economics literature attention initially focused on the first type and gradually shifted to consider the latter two – which are the most prevalent and historically significant forms of discrimination against blacks. It is ironic however that, when conservatives set out to refute discrimination, attention is seldom given any form but wage discrimination. This is not surprising since this type is more easily hidden – and we will shortly see how.

When considering discrimination of this form, it is necessary to account for differences in age, geographic location, education, job tenure, job experience and similar variables commonly included in empirical studies. Data permitting, we should go beyond present boundaries. But Sowell maintains that we must also control for cultural differences in attitudes towards education, days spent in school, quality of school resources, per-pupil expenditures, academic achievement, number of math courses taken when in high school and similar variables in order to explain current income inequality (1981, pp. 21-3).

We do not deny the importance of math preparation, for example, in expanding career options. But one can just as easily insist upon controlling for the quality of education of the math instructor or the pleasantness of the classroom environment because these factors are important also. It is not the recognition of a causal relation between such factors and income attainment that we object to. But rather we object to the insistence by conservatives that research conclusions are valid only if they account for all such variables. Ironically, their conclusions are still based more on conjecture than on empirical evidence. In fact, the validation of conservative propositions has relied mainly on the extent of national media exposure they generate and on their congruence with the current administration's political objectives, rather than on scientific investigation. But the remainder of this chapter will illustrate just how flawed many of these propositions are.

No one doubts that detailed information on personal attributes would shed light on individual achievement. But there are two problems here. First, the likelihood of finding a representative sample for which the universe of information is available is low; and even when found the quality of the data may still be questioned. Second, many of these control variables are causally related to racial discrimination, and as such we end up controlling for discrimination and searching for it simultaneously. Under such circumstances it is not surprising that it is difficult to detect. *In general, if the correlation of discrimination with a control variable is not explicitly taken into account in model construction, any measure of discrimination is correspondingly flawed.*[1] In the course of our examination we will illustrate one often neglected but obvious example of this.

A final methodological problem has to do with sample selection bias. Sowell asserts: 'In general, as education is specified progressively more finely, black–white income differences decline' (1981, p. 23). His example is as shown in Table 3.1.

Table 3.1 Black Individual Earnings as a Percentage of White Individual Earnings

	Percent
Total	63
College graduates	70
Doctorates in same field	100+

Source: Sowell, 1981, p. 23.

Table 3.1 illustrates how earnings differences disappear when we examine 'truly comparable' individuals, such as black and white PhD holders in the same field. But what has been proven here? Only that the salaries of blacks in the sample are similar to those of whites in the sample. But nothing can be concluded for blacks whose doctoral education was prevented by discrimination because they are not in the sample. This means that, by focusing only on the earnings of doctorates in the same field, we would fail to uncover the full extent of earnings discrimination associated with educational attainment.

A similar problem arises when we examine the hourly earnings of black and white workers who were 25 years of age or less in January 1983: $4.44 and $4.63 respectively. By this criterion alone whites' wages are 4.3 percent higher than blacks'. But this measures earnings differences for employed workers only. Omitted from the sample are 48 percent of black workers aged 16 to 19 and 30.6 percent of blacks aged 20 to 24 who were unemployed during the same period. This compares to unemployment rates of 21.7 percent and 14.3 percent for whites in the respective age groups. To the extent that discrimination impacts employment opportunities, the difference in hourly wages fails to fully account for it – and we have every reason to believe that the impact of discrimination is greatest upon unemployed black workers (Oaxaca, 1973, p. 694; Rees, 1986, p. 615).

In reality the number of control variables in an analysis can be increased or decreased until one is satisfied with the extent of earnings differentials. Oaxaca points out that 'A researcher's choice of control variables implicitly reveals his or her attitude toward what constitutes discrimination in the labor market' (Oaxaca, 1973, p. 699). If it turns out that there is none, as in Sowell's example of PhDs in the same field, it does not mean that discrimination does not exist. It may instead mean that the sample chosen is biased against finding it. Sowell's failure to consider sample selection bias in his discussion of the earnings of black/white PhD holders in the same field is a critical shortcoming.[2] Still, this does not mean that we should cease examining comparable individuals or stop controlling for relevant factors when investigating racial inequality; and all major studies have done so (Blinder, 1973; Corcoran and Duncan, 1979; Mincer and Polachek, 1974).

Researchers have also reached a common, if explicitly unstated, consensus on variables which should be included in studies of income discrimination. But conservatives have dismissed findings of discrimination based on these approaches and insist instead that a great deal more variables are necessary. Yet they have not conducted such empirical studies for obvious reasons. It is quite difficult to find data that are representative, current and of good quality at the very fine level of detail insisted upon by conservatives. Further, it is very doubtful that such data would alter any fundamental conclusions. Finally, if our investigations must await such data, we may never understand the nature and impact of racial discrimination or any other social phenomena for that matter.

The narrow focus on wage inequality allows conservatives to dismiss claims of discrimination by maintaining that sufficient variables have not been accounted for. But while this method of argument is well suited to wage discrimination, the other types of discrimination cannot be dismissed so easily. To account for the differentials in rates of black and white unemployment and job mobility, conservatives must revert to hypothetical logic. Specifically, firms do not discriminate in hiring and promotions in the long run because nondiscriminating firms will gain a competitive cost advantage by hiring blacks. Unemployment among blacks must therefore reflect their relative shortage of job-related attributes.

In Chapter 4 we will examine the characteristics and impacts of occupational discrimination. Additionally, we will go into greater detail on the various theories of racial discrimination, including those pertaining to disparities in employment and job mobility. But since this chapter focuses mainly upon wage discrimination, it is fitting that we make some mention of the existing methodology for measuring it.

Measuring Earnings Inequality

The most popular method of examining wage inequality is associated with the pioneering work of Gary Becker (1971 [1957]) and more recently Oaxaca (1973). Becker's purpose is to derive a coefficient of discrimination that captures the inequality in wages between black and white workers. The coefficient is a quotient of the extent of wage disparity between blacks and whites due to discrimination, divided by the total difference in wages. More specifically, it is the proportion of wage inequality unexplained once all relevant productivity differences are controlled. It is computed as follows:

$$D = \frac{W_{b'} - \bar{W}_b}{\bar{W}_w - \bar{W}_b}$$

where $\bar{W}_b$ measures the mean wages of blacks and $\bar{W}_w$ is the mean wages of whites. Similarly $W_{b'}$ represents the wages of blacks if they had the same job-related characteristics and productivity as whites. The denominator is the mean difference in wages between blacks and whites, while the numerator is the extent of difference unexplained by job-related attributes. Theoretically, job attributes have been controlled. Therefore the numerator measures wage discrimination. To estimate it we use a variety of socioeconomic variables, including education, job experience, tenure, union membership, geographic location, age and occupation, as regressors. Then we regress wages (or the natural logarithm of wages) on the vector of socioeconomic variables which includes a dummy variable for race. Once estimated, the coefficient for the race variable represents wage differences remaining after controlling for the socioeconomic variables and constitutes the numerator in our equation above. The denominator is easily determined, and the resulting quotient is the discrimination coefficient. If the resulting value is 0.55, it means that 55 percent of the difference in wages between blacks and whites is unexplained by socioeconomic variables, and we thereby attribute it to discrimination. Obviously measures of discrimination may be biased by the vector of variables included or those excluded (Greenwald, 1982, pp. 244-7).[3] Nonetheless, since conservative criticisms of this approach are central to their refutation of discrimination, we will explore such variables in great detail throughout the remainder of this chapter. We start by examining each attribute separately and then consider them collectively in a regression analysis.

Earnings, Age and Education

The first and most obvious error made by conservatives is the assertion that earnings differentials between blacks and whites are explainable in large part by the differences in age between the two populations. Sowell states:

> Perhaps the simplest way to illustrate the great impact of age on income is to point out that differences in income between age groups are even greater than racial differences in income. Families headed by persons in the 45-54-year-old bracket average 93 percent higher income than families headed by persons under 25 years of age in 1974, while white incomes the same year averaged 62 percent higher than black incomes.
>
> (1981, p. 10)

Similarly, he notes that the median age of the Jewish population is 46, the Irish median is 37, the total US population's median is 28, and blacks' median is 22. On average blacks are seven years younger than whites, and this causes them to have lower incomes (1981, p. 11).

To analyze this and other conservative propositions, we use the US Bureau of the Census *Current Population Survey* (*CPS*) microdata tapes for the month of January 1983. This particular month was chosen because the monthly survey of 71,000 households was supplemented by a survey of occupational mobility and job tenure.[4] The supplement allows researchers to determine precisely the extent and type of job training, degree of experience, tenure and many other factors that usually can only be approximated through the use of surrogate or 'instrumental variables.' For example, measures of job experience are usually approximated by subtracting years of education plus six from current age. But this supplemental questionnaire asks for the number of months and years an individual has been engaged in his or her present occupation, tenure with present employer, type of training and other questions related to one's job qualifications.

The *CPS* contains 168,124 individual records which are weighted up to get comparable totals for the entire population. We have restricted our analysis for the most part to workers who are paid by the hour. This solves many problems commonly associated with analyses of black/white annual earnings. One major problem it circumvents is the need to control for length of time worked during the year (that is, spells of unemployment). Failure to control for this biases studies of annual earnings.

The very first finding contradicts Sowell in an astonishing manner. Table 3.2 records these results and illustrates the error of assuming that the average age of the total black population is similar to that of the black working population. We see in the table that the two are not the same at all. While the median age of the total black population is six years younger than that of the white population, the median age of black employed hourly workers is two years older than that of their white counterpart. By Sowell's logic, then, black hourly workers should earn more than whites. But the mean earnings per hour for blacks and whites in 1983 were $6.05 and $6.57 respectively. The results indicate that one cannot simply attribute differences in earnings to age differences. And

Table 3.2 Median Age of the Total and Working Populations, 1983

Median age	Black	White
Employed hourly workers	33 years[a]	31 years[c]
Total population	25 years[b]	31 years[d]

[a] N = 5,696,855. [b] N = 27,096,570. [c] N = 42,388,306.
[d] N = 195,014,529.

Source: CPS microdata tapes, January 1983.

yet Sowell's treatises as well as those of some other conservatives (for example see Block and Walker, 1982) continue to repeat this erroneous proposition.

Generally, economists agree that there is a 'vintage' effect on the wage differential between black and white workers. Specifically, due to discrimination older cohorts of blacks are likely to be further behind their age peers in education, work experience and income than are younger black cohorts. But some conservatives carry this conclusion to the extreme by asserting that current income disparities are a reflection almost totally of past discriminatory practices, because younger more educated blacks have closed and in some cases even reversed the gap. According to Gilder 'The remaining gap, the evidence increasingly suggests, relates not chiefly to discrimination against blacks but to earlier discrimination against their parents and to government-induced dependency of female-headed families' (Gilder, 1981, p. 132.)[5]

Table 3.3 shows that a black earnings disadvantage exists for every age cohort except one: cohort 11, ages 65 to 69. Additionally, this disadvantage is sizable for all but two age groups: cohorts 1 and 11. The size of the earnings gap is smaller for younger cohorts but it is still rather significant, especially for cohorts 2 through 12 (excepting 11).

To examine this more systematically, we converted the information in Table 3.3 to the graphs in Figure 3.1, which gives a cross-sectional age/earnings profile of black and white workers. The figure indicates that hourly earnings for black and white cohorts are the lowest for workers less than 25 years of age, reach a maximum between ages 50-54 and are lower for older cohorts. The black/white cohort earnings gap measures partially the vintage effect on wages of past episodes of discrimination.

Table 3.3 Age and Hourly Earnings of Black and White Workers, 1983

Cohort group no.	Age definition	Hourly earnings	
		White	Black
1	less than 25	$4.63	$4.44
2	25–29	7.11	6.42
3	30–34	7.58	6.74
4	35–39	7.63	6.89
5	40–44	7.38	6.57
6	45–49	7.66	6.23
7	50–54	7.77	7.08
8	55–59	7.76	6.38
9	60–61	6.78	4.90
10	62–64	6.98	3.98
11	65–69	5.11	6.04
12	70+	5.35	4.09

Number of weighted cases = 48,085,162.

Source: CPS microdata tapes, January 1983.

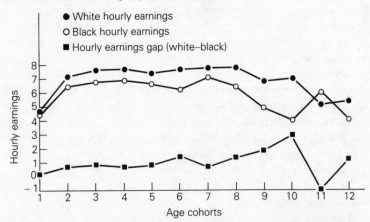

Figure 3.1 Age/earnings profile of black and white hourly workers.

Source: CPS microdata tapes, January 1983.

One of the best ways to evaluate recent trends in the age/earnings profile is to consider earnings differences between black and white workers in the 25-to-29-year category (cohort 2) relative to others. The data indicate that the black/white hourly earnings gap is not much different for this cohort than for those in cohorts 3 through 7. Further, the small gap for cohort 1 is partially deceiving because even though earnings are equalizing for black/white workers less than 25 years of age, this is precisely the category of black workers that is experiencing extraordinarily high rates of unemployment. Still, it would not be correct to completely overlook the general narrowing of the racial wage differential for younger cohorts as even a trend line fitted through the cohort earnings gap yields a positive coefficient of 0.066; although the t statistic turns out to be 0.8254 which is insignificant. The point here is that Gilder's contention, that younger more educated blacks have closed and even reversed the gap, is not supported. In fact there appears to be a phenomenon whereby greater equality in earnings are being traded off for higher rates of unemployment, particularly among young blacks (Rees, 1986, p. 615). But to carry the analysis further, we should introduce education into our discussion.

What happens when we consider educational attainment? Freeman (1976) has found that earnings differences narrow significantly for highly educated blacks. Over the last decade, significant gains were made by blacks in the area of education. For example, between 1970 and 1982 the proportion of blacks finishing high school for age cohort 25 to 34 years increased from 53 percent to 79 percent, or twice as fast for whites – see Figure 3.2. The corresponding percentage for whites increased from 76 percent to 87 percent. The proportion of blacks in the same age group completing at least one year of college increased also in comparison to whites. And although the proportion of blacks completing four years of college is still roughly half that of whites (13 percent to 25 percent), this same relation was 6 percent as compared to 17 percent in 1970 (US DOC, 1983, p. 16). Consider next how hourly earnings have changed in relation to educational attainment across three age cohorts: 25 to 34 years, 35 to 44 years and 45 to 54 years – see Table 3.4.

There is still not a clear association between age, education and earnings for hourly workers. While the earnings gap between younger age cohorts (25 to 34 years) with twelve years' schooling is currently less than that for older cohorts (age 45 to 54 years), $0.91 as opposed to $1.19, the younger cohorts' earnings difference is greater than that of cohorts 35 to 44 years. A similar situation exists for cohorts with four years' college. In fact, the middle cohort of blacks actually enjoys a $0.11 hourly earnings advantage

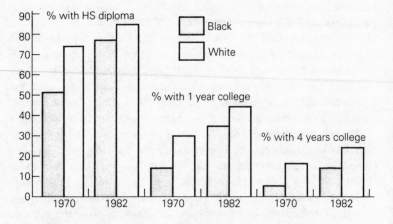

Figure 3.2 Educational attainment of blacks and whites, 1970 and 1982, age cohorts 25–34 years.

Source: CPS microdata tapes, January 1983.

Table 3.4 Hourly Earnings, Age and Educational Attainment for Blacks and Whites, 1983

| Age cohort | Education | Hourly earnings | | |
		Black	White	Gap[a]
25–34 years				
	12 yrs school	$6.24	$7.15	$0.91
	1 yr college	6.55	7.89	1.34
	4 yrs college	7.50	7.99	0.49
35–44 years				
	12 yrs school	6.99	7.47	0.48
	1 yr college	7.76	7.98	0.22
	4 yrs college	8.69	8.58	-0.11
45–54 years				
	12 yrs school	6.46	7.65	1.19
	1 yr college	8.38	8.16	-0.22
	4 yrs college	6.57	8.91	2.34

[a]Gap = white minus black hourly earnings.
Source: CPS microdata tapes, January 1983.

over whites 35 to 44 years. For blacks with one year's college the earnings gap is largest for the 25-to-34-year cohorts, followed by the 35-to-44-year cohorts, while the 45-to-54-year cohorts enjoy an earnings advantage over whites of $0.22.

We should warn that these results are for workers paid by the hour and are not necessarily consistent with annual earnings of the total population. Conceivably, the results may be biased in either direction. First, if occupational discrimination exists, restricting the job mobility of blacks to lower-status occupations, more highly qualified and experienced blacks may be crowded into waged as opposed to salaried occupations. In this case, discrimination would tend to cause an upward bias in the hourly earnings of blacks relative to whites in the same occupation. Similarly, black hourly earnings do not translate into proportionate annual earnings because of greater episodes of unemployment and less than full-time employment. As such, results based on hourly earnings understate the true annual earnings disadvantage of blacks. On the other hand, the most highly educated blacks are more likely to be salaried as opposed to hourly waged workers. In this regard, restricting the sample to hourly workers overstates the extent of discrimination because, as Freeman (1976) has shown, highly educated blacks have experienced the greatest equalization of earnings. In short, although increases in education have a strong positive effect on black earnings, the evidence does not indicate that this difference has disappeared or that it has been narrowed unambiguously to a significant extent.

Earnings and Geographical Location

Conservatives contend that much of the earnings disadvantage of blacks is actually a location disadvantage. Specifically, one-half of blacks live in the South where wages are of course much lower than in other regions.

> Mexican Americans and Puerto Ricans earn more than blacks nationally, but blacks *outside the South* earn more than either of these Hispanic groups. In short, the income advantage of these groups is neither racial nor ethnic, but locational.
>
> (Sowell, 1981, p. 23)

As indicated in Table 3.5, hourly wages are lower in the South than in the North, and blacks are most heavily concentrated in low-income divisions such as the South Atlantic, East South Central, and West South Central.[6] Alternatively, in three divisions – the East North Central, Mountain and Pacific -the average hourly wages of blacks even exceed those of whites, even though the annual

Table 3.5 Hourly Earnings by Division, Race and Sex

Division[a]	Average hourly earnings	Male		Female		Earnings gap[b]	% black in division
		Black	White	Black	White		
New England	6.08	5.97	7.05	5.22	5.10	0.48	1.9
Black	5.60						
White	6.08						
Middle Atlantic	6.68	7.22	7.81	5.86	5.51	0.13	10.1
Black	6.56						
White	6.69						
E North Central	6.91	8.22	8.34	6.76	5.47	-0.56	8.5
Black	7.42						
White	6.86						
W North Central	6.31	7.06	7.57	5.46	5.19	0.15	5.8
Black	6.17						
White	6.32						
S Atlantic	5.84	5.83	7.03	4.62	5.01	0.85	24.8
Black	5.20						
White	6.05						
E S Central	5.85	5.83	7.11	4.64	4.93	0.91	22.6
Black	5.14						
White	6.05						
W S Central	6.22	6.49	7.17	4.93	5.24	0.40	14.6
Black	5.88						
White	6.28						
Mountain	6.59	8.64	7.91	5.50	5.19	-0.29	2.7
Black	6.88						
White	6.59						
Pacific	7.42	9.63	8.57	7.00	6.09	-1.13	6.3
Black	8.48						
White	7.35						

N = 48,085,162.

[a]See the Appendix for a description of states included in each division.

[b]Earnings gap = white hourly earnings minus black hourly earnings.

Source: CPS microdata tapes, January 1983.

earnings of blacks do not exceed those of whites in any division. The table also reveals several interesting points. First, it confirms Sowell's contention that hourly earnings of black workers are lower because wages in the South are lower and blacks are concentrated there. For example, 62 percent of black hourly workers are concentrated in the three southern regions – the South Atlantic, East South Central and West South Central. While the mean hourly wage for all workers is $6.50, the mean for white Southern workers is $5.96 and for black Southern workers $5.33.

In addition to this, Table 3.5 records a pattern unnoticed by Sowell. Specifically, *black earnings are lower because the earnings disadvantage between black and white hourly workers is larger in Southern divisions.* By focusing only on wage differences between geographic locations, Sowell fails to notice and account for the earnings differential between races at these locations.

What explains this hourly earnings disadvantage or advantage experienced by blacks at specific locations? An answer to this question requires a good deal of regional analysis which is beyond the scope of the present study. But one obvious factor is that black females have an earnings advantage over white females in all divisions except those in the South. In the three southern divisions, black female hourly wages are below those of white females. Likewise, the gap between black and white male hourly workers is wider in the South Atlantic and East South Central than any other divisions and after New England, the West South Central has the next largest gap. In a separate study (Boston, 1987a) it has been demonstrated that the large earnings gap between black and white workers in the South cannot be explained by racial differences in productivities and is more likely the result of discrimination. We will see shortly that much of the earnings advantage of black females over white females is related to their greater job experience, tenure and full-time status. Yet similar factors cannot account for the earnings advantage of white males over black males.

Earnings, Experience and Occupation

Since high-level jobs require more experience and education, the underrepresentation of blacks is 'neither surprising nor proof of discrimination' according to Sowell (1981, p. 13). To Williams, a good part of the income differential between white and black male professionals may lie in occupational distribution differences between the two populations. This would imply that *even if* white and black males were paid identical incomes within an occupation, significant differences would occur when measuring median professional income.

(1982b, p. 64)

The uneven concentration of blacks in lower-paying, lower-status occupations is one focus of labor market segmentation research, and we discuss this in detail in Chapter 4. But our main contention thus far has been that *discrimination is evident not so much in wage differentials but in the differential access to employment opportunities and job mobility*. Sowell's and Williams's assertion that earnings differ because of differences in occupational distribution between blacks and whites suggests that the latter is what accounts for income inequality. Instead we argue that, if one controls for occupational distribution while examining income differences, one is actually controlling for discrimination because one of its primary forms is the relegation of blacks to low status occupations. Under these circumstances it is not surprising that any measured amount of discrimination will be smaller. Nevertheless, it is instructive to examine earnings by occupational categories and job experience. In this way we are able to get some idea of the impact of race on earnings differences across occupations.

Table 3.6 records this information and reveals the high concentration of blacks in low-status, low-paying occupations. Sixty-two percent of black males and 70.2 percent of black females are in occupations paying less than $300.00 per week. This compares to 36 percent of white males and 56.6 percent of white females. On the other hand, only 12.4 percent of black males as compared to 26.2 percent of white males are in occupations paying more than $400.00 weekly.

Table 3.7 records the hourly wages of occupations by race crossed-referenced to the average years of job experience in the occupation. Job experience was ascertained by a special *CPS* supplement which included the following question: 'Altogether, how long has . . . done the kind of work he/she is doing now?'

A number of observations can be made with respect to Table 3.7. In two occupational categories blacks enjoy an hourly earnings

Table 3.6 Major Occupation by Race and Sex, March 1984

Occupations	Black		White	
	Male	Female	Male	Female
Executive, administrative and managerial ($477)[a]	6.6	4.9	13.8	9.1
Professional ($450)	5.8	11.2	12.4	15.3
Technical and related ($388)	2.0	3.4	2.8	3.4
Skilled production and trades ($387)	14.2	2.2	20.5	2.2
Protective services ($309)	5.2	7.4	12.0	13.1
Operators, transportation and laborers ($285)	33.7	14.2	19.7	9.2
Clerical, administrative support ($273)	8.4	25.4	5.4	29.6
Service, excluding protective service and private household ($203)	15.3	24.2	6.3	15.2
Agriculture ($200)	4.3	0.5	4.6	1.1
Private household ($131)	0.4	5.9	0	1.5
Percentage in occupations with median weekly earnings:				
Above $400	12.4	16.1	26.2	24.4
Below $300	62.1	70.2	36.0	56.6

[a]The figures in parentheses are the median weekly earnings for the adjacent occupation.

Source: Children's Defense Fund, 1985, p. 63.

advantage. These are, first, technical, sales and administrative support (including sales and clerical workers) and, secondly, services (including private household and protective service workers). But these two occupational categories, along with farming, forestry and fishing, have the lowest hourly wage. In farming, forestry and fishing blacks have on average 7.45 more years of work experience than whites but earn $0.51 an hour less. In fact, a general pattern appears in the three lowest-income occupations; specifically, there

Table 3.7 Occupation by Race and Job Experience, 1983

| Occupation | Hourly earnings | | Experience | |
	Black	White	Black	White
Managerial and professional	$7.50	$8.75	5.70 yrs	7.08 yrs
Technical, sales and admin. support	6.18	5.84	4.72	5.66
Services	4.49	4.30	6.54	4.88
Production, craft and repair	8.04	9.21	7.76	9.86
Operators, fabricators and laborers	6.52	6.90	6.36	7.13
Farming, forestry and fishing	4.36	4.87	13.29	5.84

Source: CPS microdata tapes, January 1983.

does not appear to be a strong positive correlation between mean earnings by race and mean years of job experience by race.

Given the high concentration of blacks in lower-paying occupations, it is obvious that an improved distribution would reduce the earnings disadvantage with whites. On this much we agree with conservatives. Yet we differ by asserting that the adverse occupational distribution for blacks is attributable in the first place to racial inequalities both past and present.

Earnings, Sex and Occupation

Conservatives feel that their strongest evidence against interpreting difference as discrimination is provided by considering the case of women. Sowell and Williams are critical of the assertion that women earn only 59 percent as much as men because it is often taken to represent the extent of discrimination against women. Yet they point out that women remaining single earn 91 percent of the income of single men (Sowell, 1984, p. 92). Further, Gilder concludes that, 'there is very little evidence that black women suffer any discrimination at all, let alone in double doses' (1981, p. 135), and college-educated black women earn 1.25 as much as their white counterparts.

This is a curious statement because of the contradictory logic it is based upon. First, conservatives use the case of women to disprove the claim that income gaps are synonymous with discrimination – a claim that is largely a 'straw man' to begin with. Nevertheless, when black female earnings exceed those of white women, they are quick to declare this as evidence of the lack of discrimination against black women. Surprisingly, Gilder asserts this without even attempting to hold constant job-related attributes of black and white women: a shortcoming he has accused others of. Similarly, Sowell maintains that it is also impossible for male/female differences to reflect discrimination, because the

> 59 percent 'cliche' requires one to believe that employers could survive in a competitive market, paying nearly 70 percent more for given labor than they have to, whenever that labor is male. Even if employers were that needlessly generous to men, or so consumed by ideology, waste of this magnitude would be economically fatal to those businessmen who happen to have more men on the payroll than their competitors.
>
> (1984, p. 96)

Williams concludes that these facts seriously question most theories of racial earnings differentials, 'particularly the relative discrimination hypothesis' (1982, p. 58). For example, he indicates that black females have outperformed white females by a 25 percent differential, which does not imply racial discrimination against whites! Instead, he suggests, the underlying causes of this income disparity have less to do with discrimination and more to do with the greater labor force participation of black women relative to white women, a more favorable occupational distribution in comparison with white women, greater urbanization of black women relative to white women and a more equal endowment of job-related attributes (Williams, 1982a, pp. 69-75).

These factors, Williams asserts, cause earnings differences among black and white women to be nonexistent. He concludes that this casts doubts on standard explanations of black male inequality. Such explanations usually include poor-quality education, lower socioeconomic status and poor access to labor markets. But he notes that black women share the same handicaps and have advanced (1982b, p. 59).

In the assertion above, there is an unstated but mistaken presumption that black women have achieved by exerting themselves under hardships while black men have not done so and rely instead on excuses. Table 3.8 is provided to dispel this notion. It records earnings per hour, job tenure and number of hours worked per

Table 3.8 Hourly Earnings by Occupation, Sex and
Hours Worked per Week, 1983

Major occupation	Earnings per hour		Job tenure (years)		Usual hours worked per week	
	Black	White	Black	White	Black	White
Managerial and professional						
Male	$7.82	$10.51	3.3	8.0	36.8	38.6
Female	7.39	7.84	6.5	6.6	35.3	32.3
Technical, sales and admin. support						
Male	7.81	7.18	5.7	6.0	35.5	35.8
Female	5.63	5.44	4.4	5.5	34.5	32.0
Service						
Male	4.80	5.14	5.6	4.9	34.7	32.0
Female	4.29	3.76	7.1	4.9	32.1	25.6
Production						
Male	8.20	9.46	7.5	10.1	39.2	40.3
Female	5.63	5.44	10.8	6.8	38.0	37.8
Operators and laborers						
Male	7.00	7.40	6.4	7.2	38.7	37.7
Female	5.53	5.60	6.3	6.9	37.7	36.8

Source: CPS microdata tapes, January 1983.

week for black and white male and female workers. Consider the
number of hours worked per week. The table reveals that, of five
major occupations, black men work more hours per week than
white men in two: service, and operators and laborers. In a third
occupation – technical, sales and administrative support – the hours
worked per week for black and white men are virtually identical. In
the two remaining occupations – production, and managerial and
professional – white men work more hours per week than black
men. But only 18.2 percent of all blacks are in these two occupations. Therefore, a high percentage of black men and women work
more hours per week than their white counterparts. Yet this does
not convert itself into a proportionate hourly earnings advantage
or a weekly earnings advantage for black males or females.

Table 3.8 reveals that black females work significantly more
hours per week than white females in every occupation. However
this does not translate to greater relative earnings as in only three
occupations do black women enjoy hourly earnings advantages:

production, service (where 17 percent of black female hourly workers are concentrated and which includes private household work), and technical, sales and administrative support (which includes clerical workers). Despite their much longer hours of work, the average weekly earnings of black females are only $11.68 greater than those of white females, $189.60 per week as compared to $177.92 – see Table 3.9.

Black women are concentrated in the lowest-status occupations and work much longer hours than white women in all occupations. Black men are concentrated overwhelmingly in lower-status, lower-paying occupations and work more hours than white men in such occupations. For black women, this factor is reflected in a slight weekly earnings advantage over white women because many of the latter are working on a less-than-full-time basis, that is, less than 35 hours a week. For black men, this difference is not reflected in a weekly earnings advantage because the higher earnings of white men in higher-status occupations greatly overwhelm the earnings of black men in lower-status occupations (Table 3.9).

The earnings advantage of black women is certainly not evidence against discrimination. As we can see, this advantage arises from a disproportionate number of hours worked per week in comparison to white women. We therefore agree that, taken by themselves, earnings advantages and disadvantages are not evidence for or against discrimination. Thus, Gilder is absolutely mistaken in claiming that the earnings advantage of black women is evidence against discrimination. Further, Williams's attempt to dismiss standard approaches to discrimination is also flawed, because there is nothing in the evidence on black women's earnings that cannot be taken into consideration in such approaches. Once we control for the number of hours worked and other job-related attributes,

Table 3.9 Earnings by Race and Sex, 1983

	Females		Males	
	White	Black	White	Black
Weekly earnings	$177.92	$189.60	$300.59	$261.72
Hourly earnings	5.39	5.32	7.73	6.79

N = 48,085,162.

Source: CPS microdata tapes, January 1983.

77

we are then able to get a proper assessment of the amount of wage disparity between black and white women that is unexplained by such attributes.

Earnings and Family Size

Sowell argues that ethnic fertility rates play a prominent role in income differences for two reasons. First, they impact the relative age distribution of the group; and, second, they influence one's standard of living and educational possibilities. Both factors are important determinants of income (Sowell, 1981, p. 15). We have already investigated the association of age and income. Here we are interested in the relation between family size and income. Figure 3.3 examines weekly earnings of the entire work force by race

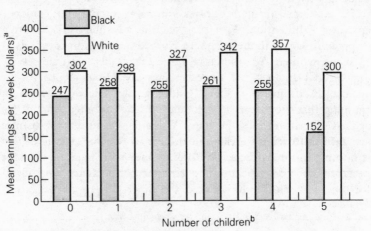

Note: Results based on total employed population.
N = 95,413,433.
[a]These are not weekly earnings of the household head but rather earnings of household workers.
[b]Number of children refers to the number in the household aged 14 years and under.

Figure 3.3 Weekly earnings by race and number of children.

Source: CPS microdata tapes, January 1983.

and number of children in the household under 14 years of age. It indicates that weekly earnings reach a maximum for households with three to four children. Secondly, the figure records the size of the racial earnings difference as family size increases. This difference widens from $55 for households with no children to $148 for those with five children. Further, the impact of family size on earnings differential is not uniform across black age cohorts. Black workers having one child in the household experience an earnings disadvantage of $65.51 if they are between 25 and 29 years and of $215.41 if between 45 and 49 years. On the other hand, blacks with four children experience a disadvantage of $53.65 if between 25 and 29 years and of $335.99 if between 45 and 49 years. Clearly, this trend indicates that something is much more powerful at reducing earnings disadvantages than simply restricting family size. This factor is obviously associated with a *time dimension*, since younger black age cohorts experience a smaller disadvantage regardless of the number of children in the household – see Table 3.10. The most important ingredient of this time dimension has been the reduction in racial discrimination as opposed to the reduction of family size.

Of course there are economic advantages associated with limiting one's family size in accordance with current and anticipated income. But we object to the proposition that has become almost axiomatic for conservatives: specifically that much of the black earnings disadvantage is attributable to high fertility rates. Economists have

Table 3.10 Weekly Earnings Difference by Number of Children and Age, 1983

| | Weekly earnings difference for age cohorts[a] | |
Number of children	25-29 yrs	45-49 yrs
0	$22.41	$115.67
1	65.51	215.41
2	23.24	151.82
3	16.05	86.81
4	53.65	335.99
5	73.04	214.60

N = 83,486,642.
[a]Difference = white minus black.

Source CPS microdata tapes, January 1983.

examined this issue, as it pertains to developing countries, for decades. We know that lower fertility rates reduce the 'dependency burden'[7] on households and society and thereby increase per capita income. But it is equally true that high incomes have a powerful negative effect upon fertility rates. In fact, high-income countries and high-income groups within countries have fertility rates so low that they barely replace the respective populations.

Do high-income groups and countries gain that status by restricting fertility rates, or is the latter a natural consequence of rising incomes? While it seems generally true that low fertility rates are a consequence of rising incomes, it does not necessarily follow that rising incomes will automatically accompany low fertility rates. In a limited sense, this is a chicken-and-egg argument that can never be fully resolved; and it is possible to provide supporting evidence for both directions of causality. But it is disturbing that conservatives have chosen to emphasize only one direction of causality – that is, low fertility rates cause higher incomes.

Within the USA the decline in birth rates accompanying rising per capita incomes has been rather dramatic. Birth rates among blacks and whites declined respectively from 34.5 and 23.8 per thousand in 1950 to 21.4 and 14.9 in 1982 – see Table 3.11. This decline has been particularly pronounced for upper-income blacks.

The continued advocacy by conservatives of the need to reduce family size in order to increase black income is not surprising. This position avoids placing any blame on the institutional factors responsible for low incomes – factors such as racial discrimination. This type of one-sided emphasis carries with it inferences of cultural and sociological deficiencies within the black community and places the burden of low incomes on blacks. While we support the need for greater family planning, particularly among youths, we insist also upon considering the whole picture. Increased efforts at family planning must complement and not substitute for continued agitation against racial inequality.

Racial Discrimination: a Comprehensive Approach

To summarize the sections above, we offer Table 3.13, which consists of regression analyses that control for variable in most

Table 3.11 Fertility Rates by Race

| | Births per 1,000 population | | |
	Black	White	Total
1955	34.5	23.8	25.0
1960	31.9	22.7	23.7
1965	27.7	18.3	19.4
1970	25.3	17.4	18.4
1975	20.7	13.6	14.8
1980	22.1	14.9	16.2
1982	21.4	14.9	16.0

Source: Children's Defense Fund, 1985, p. 114.

areas mentioned as relevant by both conservative economists and others. The final regression contains sixteen variables and includes age, job tenure, education, usual number of hours worked per week, number of children, years of work experience, geographic region, occupation and race. It is possible to conduct this analysis in a more sophisticated manner using the approach popularized by Oaxaca (1973) and employed since in several major studies including Blinder (1973), Corcoran and Duncan (1979) and Mincer and Polachek (1974). Additionally, the method is employed by Boston (1987) in a much more detailed empirical examination of the issues addressed in this chapter. But to keep the current presentation at the level of the general audience, we have avoided these more complex and less familiar methods of analysis. It should be noted that there are four regions: Northeast, South, North Central and West. The dependent variable is the natural logarithm of hourly earnings. The constant term captures the effect of working in the Northeast, with the coefficients of the remaining regional variables expressing the difference in the percent change in hourly earnings by working in the Northeast as opposed to one of the other regions. For example, equation 2 indicates that the difference in the percent change in hourly earnings varies between working in the South and in the Northeast by 6.4 percentage points. An analogous interpretation should be made for occupations. There are six in all, and the reference occupation is managerial and professional, the effect of which is also captured by the constant term. Coefficients for the remaining occupations capture the impact on hourly wages

Table 3.12 Regression Analysis

Variable	Regression results[a] (dependent variable is log of hourly earnings)		
	Equation 1	Equation 2	Equation 3
Age (years)	0.04327	0.04297	0.03651
Age squared	-0.00050	-0.00049	-0.00041
Job tenure (years)	0.01365	0.01372	0.01161
Education	0.04543	0.04381	0.03791
Usual hours worked per week	0.01365	0.01393	0.01033
Number of children in household under 14 years			0.01006
Job experience (years)	0.00677	0.00672	0.00465
Black	-0.08175	-0.04982	-0.01264
Region of country[b]			
South		-0.06442	-0.07186
North Central		0.0163	0.01441
West		0.10154	0.10237
Occupation[c]			
Technical			-0.24038
Service			-0.42132
Production			0.07433
Operators			-0.12753
Farmers			-0.32187
Constant	-0.23301	-0.21069	0.28201
Adjusted R2	0.373	0.387	0.47800
Residual degrees of freedom	47,155,871	47,155,871	47,155,865
Standard error	0.38992	0.38587	0.35605

[a]All coefficients are significant at better than the 0.01 level.
[b]Reference region is Northeast.
[c]Reference occupation is managerial, professional and administrative.

of being employed in an occupation different from the reference one. For example, equation 3 indicates that the percent change in hourly wages due to working in a service occupation as opposed to a managerial or professional occupation differs by 42.1 percentage points. Finally, the black coefficient indicates the difference in the percent change in hourly earnings for blacks as opposed to whites, where the latter is captured by the constant term. All coefficients in all three equations are significant at better than the 0.01 level.

The sign and significance of the coefficients correspond to theoretical expectations. For example, increases in education, age, job tenure and experience all positively impact the percent change in hourly wages, while the square of age has a negative coefficient. Working in the South as opposed to the Northeast negatively impacts the percent change in hourly wages, just as does working in occupations other than managerial and professional with the exception of production.

Consider next the coefficient for race. In each case the sign is negative, which is to be expected if discrimination exists. The absolute value of this coefficient represents the variation in wages that is unexplained after other job-related attributes have been controlled and represents an approximation of the impact of discrimination on hourly wages of blacks. Simply put it is the extent to which the percent change in hourly earnings of blacks is below that of whites after controlling for other factors that are in the equation. In equation 1 the coefficient is -0.0817.

The conservative argument is that as successively more factors are accounted for, the coefficient representing discrimination (actually the residual that is unexplained after all other relevant factors are controlled for) decreases almost completely. Unfortunately, they have not given a size dimension to this contention – but nonetheless we will analyze the argument as it stands.

Between column 1 and column 3 we have added successively more variables, representing job-related attributes, and examined the percent change in hourly earnings due to race. In equation 1 we do not control for the number of children, geographic region and occupation. The difference in the race coefficient is -0.08175. That is, the percentage changes in black hourly earnings are 8.17 percentage points below whites. When geographic regions are added as control variables in equation 2 the racial differential is lower as the coefficient increases to -0.04982, meaning that the estimated impact of discrimination is reduced. Finally, when variables representing the number of children and occupation are added, the coefficient increases even further to -0.01264. This last equation means, assuming all other factors are specified correctly, that discrimination lowers the percent change in hourly wages for blacks, relative to whites, by 1.26 percentage points. Occupational distribution has a large impact upon the change in hourly earnings. Once accounted for in the equation, the discrimination coefficient is reduced significantly. But does this mean that racial differences in wages have disappeared as contended by conservatives? *Absolutely not!*

In the first place we must keep in mind that we are examining hourly wages for employed workers. In this regard, the equation says nothing about the comparative earnings of two million black workers who are disproportionately unemployed or the disproportionate share of black workers who are discouraged and therefore no longer in the labor force. This means that there is some obvious sample selection bias, because the workers whose earnings are likely to be impacted the most by discrimination are not in the sample.

There is however an even more compelling problem. Equation 3 assumes that we are controlling for the occupation of workers and then examining the impact of race. Hence, when we netted out the effect of differentials in occupational distribution between blacks and whites on hourly earnings, the race coefficient dropped from -0.0498 to -0.0126. But what is actually happening here? We are netting out not only the impact of differentials in occupational distribution between blacks and whites, but along with it discrimination itself. In other words, we have argued that *the main manifestation of racial discrimination is not differential wages paid to equally productive black and white workers, but rather the differential access to employment and differing rates of occupational mobility.* If this is so, it is impossible in regression equation 3 to control for the effects of occupational differences independently of the impact of race. Stated differently, controlling for occupation is comparable to controlling for discrimination, especially if they are highly correlated. In the case of equation 3, the result has been to reduce the size of the discrimination coefficient.

If there is a relationship between discrimination and occupational distribution, multicollinearity and/or simultaneous equation bias exists between the occupation and race variables, and hence their sizes are not accurate measures of their effects.

To confirm this we constructed a test to determine the association between occupational location and race when all other job-related attributes are controlled. Before discussing this approach, however, one observation can be made on the basis of the results obtained in the regression analysis. Specifically, when equation 3 is created by introducing occupation variables into equation 2, the T statistic for the race coefficient (black) changes from -278.23 to -75.70, or decreases in statistical significance. This reflects an increase in the variance of the race coefficient and is one possible sign of multicollinearity (Pindyck and Rubinfeld, 1981,p. 89). But to examine our hypothesis more directly – that is, that discrimination relegates blacks to lower-status occupations, we constructed a logit response model.[8]

Forty-five occupations are classified as secondary or primary according to whether they require general or specific labor skills.[9] Secondary occupations generally include low-skill, lowpaying jobs, while primary occupations are just the opposite. After controlling for all job-related attributes, we would like to know if blacks are less likely to hold primary-sector jobs. This gives a testable structure to one of our most important hypotheses.

To test this, we constructed a logit response model for males ages 40 to 44. The dependent or predicted variable is the logarithm of the probability of holding a job in the primary sector. The explanatory variables are a person's race (Black), age (Age), age squared (Agesq), usual number of hours worked per week (Ushrswh), years of education (Highed), job tenure or length of time with present employer (Lpreempl), job experience (Hlngwk) and geographic region (where North Central = Ncentrl, South = South, West = West, and the reference region is North). Table 3.13 records the results of this analysis.

Table 3.13 Logit Analysis

Variable name	Coefficient	Coefficient/SE
Black	-0.51365	-3.42162
Age	-0.13673	-0.05765
Agesq	0.00181	0.06396
Ushrswh	0.00405	0.68288
Highed	0.15526	7.96389
Lpreempl	0.00341	0.49543
Hlngwk	0.00223	0.33541
Ncentrl	0.21521	1.60835
South	0.06562	0.59461
West	0.17596	1.25052
Intercept	5.54496	0.11148

Note: The logit procedure used adds 5 to the intercept and divides the logit by 2.

The region variables are referenced to the North, meaning that the coefficients of the three other regions record the probability of being in the primary sector if one lives in a region other than the North. For example, the log of the odds of being in the primary sector is greater in the North Central (0.21521), South (0.0656) and West (0.17596) than in the North. However, none of these regional coefficients are significant at the 0.05 level.

The variables that are most significant and have the greatest impact upon the probability of being in the primary sector are race (Black) and years of education (Highed). Education has the highest coefficient to standard error ratio (7.964) and positively influences the probability of being in the primary sector; its coefficient is 0.15526. Race is the next most significant variable and has a strong negative influence on the probability of being in the primary sector. Its coefficient value is -0.5136. All other variables are insignificant at the 0.05 level. The size, sign and significance of the coefficient for race strongly support our hypothesis on discrimination. Specifically, all other factors constant, blacks have a much greater probability of being in low-status, low-paying occupations.

The best way to interpret the coefficient results is to examine the probability generated by a particular set of values of our explanatory variables. Suppose we have two workers differing only by race: one black and the other white. Apart from this all other factors are the same. Specifically, they both are 42 years of age, work 40 hours per week, have 13 years of education, 5 years' tenure with present employer, 4 years' job experience in present occupation and currently reside in the North Central. Under these circumstances, the probability of a white holding a primary-sector job is 81.2 percent while that of a black is 60.7 percent. There is clearly an occupational accessibility difference attributable to race – something we will explore in greater detail in Chapter 4.

The key point is that the endogenous relationship between occupational distribution and race causes estimates of discrimination, as measured by the race variable, to be inefficient. Under these circumstances, when measured discrimination in Table 3.12 decreased from -0.0498 in equation 2 to -0.0126 in equation 3, this is to be expected. That is, by introducing occupations into the equation we are controlling for the most prevalent form of discrimination and thereby eliminating it *a priori* from the results.

In summary, as we add more and more control variables, it is true that the size of the discrimination coefficient is reduced, but certainly not enough to justify a contention that discrimination is not a significant factor in contemporary labor markets. Our results show (see equation 2 of Table 3.12) that, if one is black, the percent change in hourly wage will be below that of whites. Likewise, Table 3.13 reveals that equally qualified blacks have a 20 percent lower probability than whites of working in the primary sector. These are clear manifestations of racial inequality.

When faced with such evidence, conservatives will usually deny they have ever maintained that discrimination has disappeared. Instead, they assert, it is only 'more apparent than real' (Sowell, 1981, p. 24). But again, such a vague statement cannot constitute the basis of scientific inquiry. How much more apparent than real is it?

Color versus Culture

One of Sowell's most often repeated arguments states that West Indians have advanced further than US blacks. Therefore, color discrimination cannot be the basis of differential economic achievement.

> Black West Indians living in the United States are a group physically indistinguishable from black Americans, but with a cultural background that is quite different. If current employer racial discrimination is the primary determinant of below-average black income, West Indians' incomes would be similarly affected. Yet West Indian family incomes are 94 percent of the US national average, while the family incomes of blacks as a group are only 62 percent of the national average. West Indian 'representation' in professional occupations is double that of blacks, and slightly *higher* than that of the US population as a whole.
>
> (1984, p. 77)

Despite its popularity and the fact that it is repeated constantly by conservatives, this argument is logically flawed. In the first place, we have devoted this chapter to the conservative criticism that economists have not accounted for enough relevant variables in analyzing racial discrimination. Yet Sowell makes this comparison between US blacks and 'West Indian blacks' by controlling for only one single variable. Were we to model his argument, it would look as follows:

$$\text{Income} = a + b \text{ (West Indian)} + Ei$$

In this case the sample includes only US blacks and West Indian blacks. In the equation, West Indian is a dummy variable for ethnic group which is set to 0 if the observation is on a US black and 1 otherwise and Ei is a stochastic error term. No other factors are accounted for, not even the fact that West Indians are more concentrated in higher-income metropolitan areas and have a selective migration pattern. Sowell briefly mentions migration selectivity but fails to discuss its impact.

Migration selectivity is measured by comparing the immigrant characteristics with those of the origin population. Generally, international migration to the USA from Third World countries is highly selective of the most educated, skilled and qualified individuals. This includes scientists, engineers, academicians and doctors. Indeed, this has led to the pressing problem of the international 'brain drain' – the magnitude of which is given in Table 3.14.

The numbers for the years 1967 to 1973 are staggering when one considers that they are annual flows. To what extent is selectivity true for West Indians? Unfortunately, we do not have the answer to this question. But neither does Sowell account for it in his analysis. As such, we do not know if the higher relative earnings of West Indians are impacted by migration selectivity, but we have reasons to believe they are. Interestingly, the unemployment rate in Britain among West Indian males and white British males was 29 percent and 11.5 percent respectively in 1984 (Sinclair, 1987). Of course the migration of West Indians to Britain has not been as selective.

A second criticism has to do with the logic of the comparison. Presumably the purpose of it is to demonstrate that racism has not impeded another black ethnic group of a different culture from

Table 3.14 Annual Gross Immigration of Professional and Technical Personnel from Developing Countries into the USA

Year	Number of persons[a]
1967	23,361
1968	28,511
1969	27,536
1970	33.796
1971	38,647
1972	39,106
1973	31,939
1961-76:	
Physicians and surgeons	40,876
Engineers and scientists	77,279

[a]Included in this category are engineers, natural and social scientists, surgeons, physicians and technical worker.

Sources: Todaro, 1982, p. 320; Fatani, 1981, pp. 40-3.

advancing. However, the nature of this cross-cultural comparison is suspect because so many factors vary across cultures. But why compare black Americans with West Indians in the first place? Why not restrict the comparison to blacks by simply identifying a sample of blacks that have experienced significant racial oppression and another sample whose racial experiences have been less severe? If (other things being equal) racial discrimination does not impact the achievement of blacks then the economic advancement or stagnation of both groups should be similar.

We have seen, however, that racism does impact black advancement, and it is unnecessary to examine West Indians, Chinese, or other ethnic groups to prove or disprove this. Consider the rapid progress of the new black capitalist class and the new black middle class. Their greater achievement is due to the smaller impact that racial discrimination has upon their life chances. On the other hand, the stagnation of the old black capitalist and middle classes is due to the greater impact of racial subjugation. In short, some blacks have experienced lesser degrees of racism and advanced much further. Others have experienced more racism and stagnated to a greater extent. Nevertheless all are from the same ethnic group, and thereby historical, cultural, political and other factors are similar and do not impact the outcome of the analysis. This is a more sound analysis.

Approaching the issue in this manner forces conservatives to abandon their inferred notions of black cultural deficiency. In fact, the methodological structure and logical consequence of Sowell's approach are reminiscent of the 'culture of poverty' propositions that have long since been refuted (Barrera, 1979, pp. 174–84). While this does not appear to be his intended purpose, it is the logical outcome of his approach. We agree with Sowell's assertion that

> Blacks are indeed a special case. But to say that blacks literally cannot be compared to other groups is to say that we must remain ignorant of how much that special history has to do with contemporary social phenomena. Or else we must accept foregone conclusions based on a vision rather than on facts.
>
> (Sowell, 1984, p. 76)

Yet no one has said that it is impossible to draw valuable lessons from other ethnic groups. But in so doing, we must certainly consider more factors than the similarity in skin color.

The Chinese, we are told, suffered a worse oppression than blacks and have done better, while blacks in Brazil have suffered less oppression and done worse than US blacks (Sowell, 1984, p. 74). Therefore, Sowell concludes, the degree of oppression does not necessarily correspond to the degree of disadvantage, and a unique history does not necessarily translate into a unique position vis-a-vis the national average. This is indeed a strange argument, since no one has said that there exists a unique correspondence between the degree of oppression and the degree of disadvantage. We have asserted only that the disadvantage currently experienced by blacks can be traced to racial inequalities both past and present. Beyond this it is quite impossible to compare in any reasonable manner degrees of oppression and degrees of disadvantage across ethnic groups. Furthermore, who is to say which group is more oppressed?

Consider the hypothetical case of two slaves; one is brutalized frequently but educated properly, and the other is treated benevolently but miseducated thoroughly. Which person is worse off upon gaining freedom? This only illustrates how meaningless observations on relative brutality are. Sowell claims: 'The number of Chinese killed within a few days, at various times in the history of southeast Asia, has on a number of occasions exceeded all the blacks ever lynched in the history of the United States' (1984, p. 22). Even if predisposed to do so, how are we to evaluate such a statement? Should we consider the death rate cause by oppression relative to the sizes of the two populations, or the cruelty of each death? Should we include or exclude the African slave trade? No matter how one chooses to define degrees of oppression, it is obviously impossible to make relevant cross-cultural comparisons based upon it.

In fact, much of this argument is a 'straw man' because we have not claimed that a certain degree of disadvantage is correlated with a given degree of oppression. Nor have we asserted that it is impossible for an ethnic minority, confronted with discrimination, to advance economically. In fact, larger and larger segments of blacks are doing it every day – and we demonstrated how and why in Chapter 2. Instead, we have maintained only that the economic disadvantage of blacks in the USA is causally related to racial discrimination. In saying this, we do not discard the valuable experiences of other minorities, but recognize the need to interpret such experiences within the unique historical environment giving rise to them.

Conclusions

The issue, as Sowell understands it, 'is not whether any discrimination exists. The issue is whether what is used as evidence is in fact evidence' (1984, p. 127). But in truth the issue is whether discrimination exists, since conservatives have gone to great lengths in attempting to disprove it. Yet they have failed. Factors such as age, education and geographical location are important in relative income comparisons. But discrimination is equally important and cannot be dismissed, as conservatives would have us do. The standard approach to measuring income inequality places a heavy premium upon identifying and correctly measuring job-related attributes. Yet most noted empirical studies have sufficiently done so. Finally, the conservative accusation that discrimination research 'has been based on anecdotal evidence and emotional reference to earlier periods' (Block and Walker, 1982, p. 15) is true – but for the accusers (that is, conservatives) rather than the accused.

Notes Chapter 3

1 This is an econometric problem of both multicollinearity and simultaneous equation bias.
2 See, for example, Sowell, 1981, pp. 23-4.
3 Oaxaca's (1973) method is more efficient at disaggregating the explained and unexplained portions of the wage differential and correlating these to their respective socioeconomic characteristics. But in order to keep the presentation as simple as possible we avoid using this approach and refer interested readers to Boston (1987b) for an application of this method to many of the issues discussed in this chapter.
4 For a detailed description of the tapes, see *Current Population Survey*, January 1983, Technical Documentation, Data User Services Division, Bureau of the Census, Washington, DC; and Bureau of the Census, *The Current Population Survey: Design and Methodology*, Technical Paper 40, US GPO, Washington, DC.
5 It is interesting to note that while conservatives acknowledge the existence of past discrimination, they reject any cumulative causal link between it and contemporary inequality. Yet when the discussion turns to poverty, welfare dependency, family instability and so-called 'social pathologies' of blacks, conservatives never cease emphasizing intergenerational transmission and cumulative causation. This type of methodological eclecticism is also present in approaches to other major issues.
6 See the Appendix for a listing of the states within each division.
7 By the 'dependency burden' we commonly refer to the proportion of a population falling in the ages of 0 to 15 and 64 and over. In many developing countries the population under 15 accounts for half of the total population and must rely upon resources generated by the productive labor force.
8 This model will be explained in much greater detail in Chapter 4. Here we present only a small sample of the results obtained.
9 A precise definition and methodological explanation of this classification scheme is given in Chapter 4. However, we should mention that it avoids many of the problems typically encountered when attempting to segment the labor force, particularly the problem of truncation bias.

4 Segmented Markets, Discriminated Labor

> The most distinctive characteristic of the Negro's position in the world of labor is his relegation to occupations in which he does not compete with white workers – in short, the perpetuation of the tradition of black men's and white men's jobs. This tradition is not confined to the South, but extends throughout the country.
>
> (Spero and Harris, 1931, p. 180)

Chapter 3 demonstrated that racial wage discrimination persists in contemporary labor markets. Yet wage discrimination is not the fundamental form of labor market inequality faced by blacks. More fundamentally, there exist inequalities in employment opportunities, in job status and promotions and in occupational mobility. Although half a century old, the observation above made by Spero and Harris has much relevance today.

This chapter is centered on an explication of occupational discrimination and addresses the following questions. To what extent are labor markets segmented such that some workers' employment opportunities are concentrated among 'good jobs' while others are concentrated among 'bad jobs'? Are blacks more likely to be in the segment consisting of 'bad jobs,' assuming all other job-related attributes are held constant? Finally, what is the extent of mobility between segments, and does this vary by race?

The economics of labor market segmentation (LMS) provides a means of answering these questions, and this chapter is devoted to a detailed investigation of this theory's central hypotheses. In the process, we will understand more fully the fundamental form of discrimination in contemporary labor markets. Yet for all its

93

usefulness in race/class analyses, LMS theory must first be purged of its conservative integument. In particular, we challenge the theory's explanation of the behavior of secondary-sector workers. But this, along with many other issues, is examined in detail below.

The modern focus on segmented labor markets arose more than a decade after Becker's seminal analysis of wage discrimination (1957). Influenced by early analyses of Balkanized labor markets, by Bergman's examination of occupational crowding (1971), by Doeringer and Piore's work on dual labor markets (1971) and by subsequent studies of segmented labor markets (Bluestone, 1970; Edwards, Reich and Gordon, 1975), economists' preoccupation with wage discrimination began to shift.[1] Stiglitz puts pre-segmentation approaches in their clearest perspective.

> The central problem posed by the economics of discrimination is the following: Under what circumstances is it possible for groups with identical economic characteristics to receive different wages in a market equilibrium? If people of the same productivity receive different wages, then there are profits to be made by hiring the low wage individual. If all firms are profit maximizers, then all will demand the services of the low-wage individual, bidding their wages up until the wage differential is eliminated. Why does this not occur?
>
> (Stiglitz, 1973, p. 287)

According to Marshall (1974), theoretical attempts to resolve this contradiction produced mechanical results that lacked congruence with reality (see related criticisms by Alexis and Medoff, 1984; Darity, 1982; Reich, 1981).

The shortcomings of the early theories led economists in three divergent directions. One group sought to explain inequality by focusing upon factors external to the labor market but which nonetheless impacted the quality of black labor supplied. These 'supply-side' theories covered a wide array of issues believed to be responsible for contemporary inequality – including so-called deficiencies in black culture, the black family, black social structure and 'ghetto pathologies.' There were also supply-side theories which concentrated less on internal causation and deficiency and more on social structural and institutional discrimination in areas such as education.[2]

A second group turned its attention to the characteristics of labor markets and the relative demand for and position of blacks within them. This approach, associated with LMS theory, sees qualitative differences in the labor markets of various firms and occupations. Such differences are believed to perpetuate a low-wage, low-status secondary sector alongside a more prestigious high-wage primary labor market segment.

Finally, conservative economists adopted a third and altogether different approach. While neoclassical economists were preoccupied with explaining the theoretical compatibility of wage inequality and competitive labor market equilibrium, conservatives simply dismissed all such attempts. Instead, they maintained that the inexorable force of competition in unfettered labor markets will reduce over time all differences in wages to real differences in human capital attributes between black and white workers. As such, they claim that contemporary labor market differentials across race are based not on discrimination but on differences in skills and qualifications.

To neoclassical economists, discrimination exists when individuals 'with the same economic characteristics receive different wages' because of racial or religious differences (Stiglitz, 1973, p. 287). The amount of discrimination is determined by calculating the size of the discrimination coefficient. Current computations for the USA using 1976 data indicated that the coefficient is about 50 percent (Greenwald, 1982, p. 246). In a very exhaustive study by Corcoran and Duncan (1979), this coefficient (i.e. the unexplained residual once other factors are controlled) is determined to be 47 percent.

According to Becker's theory, whites dislike associating with blacks and have the ability to institute such feelings through labor market arrangements. When firms practice employment discrimination, only white workers are hired, even if they must be paid wage premiums. If the work force is integrated, white workers must be paid a premium to work alongside blacks. Finally, if the distaste for working with blacks is strong enough, white workers will even accept lower wages to remain separate. 'If an individual has a "taste for discrimination," he must act as if he were willing to pay something, either directly or in the form of reduced income, to be associated with some persons instead of others' (Becker, 1957, p. 14).

As noted earlier, this theory has been subjected to many criticisms, most of which are so well known we will not bother to repeat them here. For our purposes however the most important criticism is the theory's inability to explain long-run differences in wages (assuming equal worker productivities and competitive labor markets) without resorting to unrealistic assumptions.

Exploiting this weakness, conservatives insist that discrimination and competitive equilibria are incompatible. Since the latter exist, they contend, discrimination cannot. To Sowell, the costs associated with discrimination correspond to a downward sloping demand curve – meaning that the higher the costs the less likely will discrimination be indulged in. These costs take the form of forgone opportunities to make money. The less discriminatory transactor will 'acquire a competitive advantage, forcing others either to reduce their discrimination or to risk losing profits, perhaps even being forced out of business' (1981, p. 26). In short, the price of discrimination tends to limit its extent, and by conservative logic the racial motivations of white employers are irrelevant. Their profit-seeking activities will unwittingly reduce all unjustified income differences. There is, then, a tendency for the 'self-interested action of profit seekers to ensure that persons who are subject to discrimination will not suffer financially from this affliction' (Block and Walker, 1982, p. 10).

Within the neoclassical paradigm, criticisms of Becker's approach led to the creation of a theory of inequality more compatible with competitive equilibrium. This Arrow-Phelps approach (Arrow, 1972a, 1972b, 1974; Phelps, 1972) sees discrimination evolving out of mistaken perception and imperfect information that white employers have on the productivities of black workers. Such perceptions supposedly lead employers to hire blacks only at lower wages or not at all. Blacks and whites are assumed to have equal average productivities, but blacks, have greater variance and their true productivity is more difficult and costly to measure. Because employers want to rank prospective employees, they must develop a proxy for the productivity of blacks. Because of the belief that blacks as a group have a wider variance in productivity or even lower average productivity, whites are more likely to be hired. The hypothesis is centered on the behavior of risk-averse employers who believe 'it is much more costly to make the mistake of hiring an inefficient worker than to make the mistake of passing over a productive one' (Reich, 1981, p. 104). This leads employers to rank blacks lower in the employment queue than whites.

Marshall (1974, p. 861) has asked a crucial question in this regard. That is, what happens when an employer's perception of blacks is proven false by accurate information – and yet blacks are still confronted with employment discrimination? According to the theory, competition should force perceptions in line with reality, causing discrimination to wither away and forcing all employment and wage differences in line with real productivity differences. But since Marshall believes that discrimination persists in labor markets, even though employers possess correct information on the capabilities of blacks, his comment is meant as a criticism of this variation of neoclassical theory. Ironically, this reasoning has led conservatives to derive the opposite conclusion. Where Arrow's intent is to explain how discrimination can persist in competitive markets, conservatives have appropriated this same argument in an attempt to demonstrate the impossibility of it. As stated by Sowell (1981, p. 28):

> Where the perception of the whole group's average performance level is incorrect, several things would tend to happen in a market economy. First, those transactors with more accurate assessments would gain a competitive advantage over those more blinded by prejudice or inertia. This puts a cost on misperceptions, just as there is a cost on discrimination based on pure bigotry. The magnitude of this cost would vary with the degree of competitiveness of the relevant market. The more competitive the market, the more the costs approach a prohibitive level. In a highly competitive market, any firm paying more for a factor of production, such as labor, could have its survival jeopardized.

Sowell concludes that the belief that 'group perceptions are misperceptions' is an arbitrary premise which runs counter to the process of economic analysis. Block and Walker (1982) contend that, even where such forms of discrimination exist, it is justified because employers are not 'duty bound' to invest in enough information to determine the true productivities of all job applicants just to ensure that bias results do not occur. Instead, firms invest only to the point at which the marginal cost of additional information is justified by the additional revenue it produces. They further maintain that race and sex are cheaply identifiable characteristics which are highly correlated with workers' productivity and therefore may be used as proxy variables (1982, pp. 19-20). The major premise of conservatives then is that market competition eradicates all forms of racial inequality. But is this true in reality?

Political Economy of Discrimination

In Chapter 2 we discussed the interplay of politics, economics and inequality. It was emphasized that every major improvement in the economic status of blacks was caused by coercive political intervention rather than by free market forces. For example, it was only under force that the system of slavery was abolished. But even following the demise of this institution, a system of 'Black Codes' and 'contract labor' was established which was in many ways equally harsh on blacks. Still, the collapse of contract labor did not come through market competition and the free flow of resources. In fact, 'Black Codes,' the legal superstructure of the contract labor system, were instituted by property owners with the intended purpose of restricting the free flow of black workers among alternative labor markets. Once again, political intervention in the form of Reconstruction governments in the South was necessary to eradicate this system and the gross inequalities it imposed upon blacks. Tenant farming relations evolved out of the defeat of Reconstruction, and under this system blacks became sharecroppers overwhelmingly. But this hybrid stage, between modern wage labor relations and slavery, still did not allow the full and free flow of black labor between competing markets. While Jim Crow laws constrained the mobility and economic rewards of black tenant farmers, landowners entrapped them in an almost inescapable web of debt peonage. It was often the case that, under this system, an increase in productivity and efficiency resulted in greater debt on the part of the sharecropper – because the landlord always attempted to hold in debt the most productive and efficient tenant farmers. Johnson, Embree and Alexander observed:

The very qualities which might normally lead a tenant to attain the position of renter, and eventually owner, are just the ones which make him a permanent asset as a cropper. Landlords, thus, are most concerned with maintaining the system that furnishes them labor and that keeps this labor under their control, that is, in the tenancy class.

(1935, p. 20)

Massive black out-migration from the South was the response to these circumstances. Decades later, the Civil Rights Movement provided the political impetus for the collapse of Jim Crow segregation. Once again, coercion (in the form of the Civil Rights and Black Power movements) was necessary to obtain greater mobility of black labor and capital resources. When *de jure* segregation was outlawed, the maintenance of pure wage discrimination became increasingly difficult. Yet occupational segmentation of blacks persists and is currently represented by unjust inequalities in hiring, promotions and job status. As in the past, there is no reason to believe that market competition will cause such inequalities to disappear automatically. Instead, history has shown that either government intervention or the intervention of external political forces is a prerequisite for greater black equality.

The historical account just given clearly indicates that racial subjugation, whether during slavery or the Jim Crow era, preserved the existing socio-economic order. But this is not just true for the USA. Consider how Britain governed its former colonial territories. In Africa, India and other places under British domination, colonial administrators as well as executives of colonial enterprises were British nationals and not indigenes – even though the former were paid large wage premiums and qualified indigenous talent was available. In fact, the latter usually possessed training from British universities. Given this, why did employers (even though driven by the profit motive) allow such wage premiums to exist in colonial territories? Analogously, why today does South Africa rely almost exclusively on whites to supervise and administer corporations and the government when a large pool of qualified black South Africans are available at lower wages – many trained in the USA and Britain? Why has not the profit motive eliminated wage premiums based on race?

One might contend that these are not competitive situations. Pure market forces have been impaired by political interests and motivations. This is precisely correct; they are not perfectly competitive situations. But they are real world situations, and in the real world political interest and economic arrangements are far from mutually exclusive.

Firms do attempt to maximize profits, whether in the short or the long run. They also attempt to optimize their competitive position vis-a-vis other firms – which often leads to mergers, acquisitions and noncompetitive markets. But these two factors alone are not sufficient to fully explain the persistence of unjustified racial wage premiums in competitive or quasi-competitive labor markets. The reason is that, collectively, firms are also interested in establishing and maintaining socioeconomic arrangements most amenable to the fulfillment of profit maximization. Such arrangements cover a wide spectrum of possibilities including practices and policies which alternately free the market and further restrict it. A good example of this is the advocacy by firms of increased import restrictions at times and free trade at others. Likewise, on occasion firms are staunch supporters of market regulation while on other occasions they strongly support deregulation. In South Africa the social order most compatible with white domination is apartheid. In a past era of US history, Jim Crow segregation represented an analogously compatible social order. But under either social order, it is extremely naive to believe that pure market forces can eliminate racial inequality.

Competitive optimality in this sense involves a trade-off among three objectives: profit maximization, competitive advantage and an amenable social order. Since firms operate on a self-interested basis, it is often the government that must reconcile the common interests, even at the expense of sacrificing profits for some. By optimizing over three objectives, the existence of racial wage premiums may or may not be compatible with competitive equilibrium. Further, there is no reason to believe that wage or occupational discrimination will automatically disappear without political coercion or market interference – especially if the maintenance of a given socioeconomic arrangement overrides profit maximization as a short-run motive.

This describes the world as it actually exists even if it does not fit neatly into the neoclassical or conservative paradigm of competitive equilibrium. Discrimination against blacks is a fact. However, it is less clear whether an instance of it can be shown to exist in a market where all resources are freely mobile. This is because the history of black inequality in the USA is largely one of various forms of restricted mobility of black labor. In this regard, it is clear that economic interests themselves have encumbered market operations; and to speak of a free market is indeed an abstraction. So the relevant question is not whether markets are free of political interest, but rather whose interest do they serve? This is an appropriate setting for entering into our next topic on segmented labor market – the major contemporary vehicle of black labor inequality.

Segmented Labor Markets: Initial Hypothesis

There are essentially two theses on the evolution of segmented labor markets. The first argues that segmented markets emerged during the transformation of the economy from its competitive stage to its current monopoly stage (Wachtel, 1975). The second, which is a revision of the first, contends that segmentation is the outcome of an interaction between long swings in economic activity, social structures of accumulation and the organization of work and labor markets corresponding thereto (Gordon, Edwards and Reich, 1982, pp. 1-17). In both cases, a main objective is to determine if there exist qualitatively distinct sectors of labor, restricted inter-sectoral mobility and a disproportionate and unfair relegation of certain types of labor (for example, black or female) to the least favorable sector. Although the initial focus of labor market segmentation (LMS) theory centered on explaining the disadvantaged position of black labor, this has changed over time (Piore, 1975, p. 125).

Segmented labor markets, according to the original thesis, evolved out of structural changes occurring in the economy at an advanced stage of development. More specifically, it is maintained that the emergence and dominance of monopoly corporations at the turn of the century divided the economy into two distinct segments: a primary segment and a secondary one. This transition, which occurred between 1890 and 1920, changed a more or less open, competitive, local-market-oriented economy to one dominated by closed oligopolies with international orientations. Firms

101

in the primary segment are distinguishable by their greater size, organizational structure, industrial location, market concentration and power, ability to adapt to a changing environment, factor endowment and extent of conglomeration (Edwards, Reich and Gordon, 1975; Kalleberg, Wallace and Althauser, 1981, pp. 653-4).

This differs from secondary sector firms, which are competitive, exercise no autonomous influence over market prices and are typically involved in a single product line or a series of related products. According to Edwards, Reich and Gordon, the emergence of oligopolistic industries led to a reorganization of the structure of the firm to suit its new economic scale. 'Simple hierarchy' of the competitive firm, which is characterized by 'arbitrary, highly visible, direct command rule by superiors over subordinates,' was replaced by a system of 'bureaucratic control' characterized by a new invisible system of hierarchical authority embedded in the organizational structure of the firm (1975, pp. xi-xxi). This structure placed increased emphasis on status distinctions among jobs and established criteria to evaluate workers' performances rather than the arbitrary evaluation of supervisors. Along with this there emerged an impersonal work environment that was less conducive to workers' militancy, and where union demands were no longer centered on control over work but rather on issues of wages, benefits and other procedural matters. This altered focus further legitimized the new system of bureaucratic control.

These factors, associated with the presence of internal labor markets, are believed to have given rise to the primary sector. The internal labor market differs from the general market in the way in which job vacancies are filled. Rather than through openly competitive labor markets, vacancies in internal markets are filled through internal job bidding, promotions, evaluation procedures and training and development programs. This essentially restricts vacancies to the firm's existing work force (Althauser and Kalleberg, 1981, pp. 121-3; Doeringer and Piore, 1971).

It is apparent that internal labor markets differ from traditional labor markets because in the latter such vacancies are filled through the open bidding of competing potential employers with competing potential workers.

Evolution of the internal market is viewed both as a response to technical demands of oligopolistic corporations and as a political and strategic response by corporate owners and managers to a growing labor militancy. Within this context, the imposition of hierarchical job categories and the fostering of racial, ethnic and sexual antagonisms are viewed as part of a depoliticizing process, ultimately leading to a divided labor movement (Wachtel, 1975).

The need for such a strategy is believed to have emerged as follows. More than a century ago, during the competitive stage of capitalism, the factory system evolved and eliminated many skilled craft occupations, forcing skilled workers to seek employment in relatively undifferentiated, unskilled jobs. Such workers are appropriately referred to as the homogeneous labor force, and Edwards, Reich and Gordon (1975) trace the development of this process. Increasingly, homogenization of the work force brought large numbers of workers together for the first time in giant corporations and created and intensified labor conflict. As monopoly corporations emerged at the turn of the century, this growing labor militancy threatened their interests. To meet this growing challenge, employers fostered segmentation to 'divide and conquer' the labor force.

Within the firm, job ladders were created with definite entry-level positions as well as definitive patterns of promotion. Outside the corporation, the hiring of workers from rival nationalities to strike-break created ethnic antagonisms (Reich, Gordon and Edwards, 1973, p. 361). Again, it is believed that such practices were designed to reinforce the existing system of control by preventing united actions among workers. Segmented markets then are perceived as the outcome of the struggle between employers and labor for control over the workplace (Wallace and Kalleberg, 1981, p. 85). This conflict resulted in the mitigation of workers' class consciousness and the diminution of the power of labor unions.

Although this scenario has a great deal of intuitive appeal and is correct in many respects, one immediate problem it poses is the lack of a clearly defined conception of market segmentation. Specifically, do segments cut across industries, occupations, gender, race, or some combination of these? Unfortunately, this problem has yet to be sufficiently resolved in the literature.

The existence of internal markets in the primary sector provides higher wages and greater employment stability. There are three features common to corporations in the primary sector. (1) Their large size permits them increasingly to fill vacancies through internal mechanisms. (2) The increased differentiation of job categories and corresponding status positions associated with bureaucratically controlled firms increases the possibility and desirability of upward movement within the firm. And (3) the greater cyclical stability of these forms means that fewer labor force adjustments are necessary and the demand for labor is more stable (Edwards, Reich and Gordon, 1975, p. 6).

On the other hand, competitive firms, which LMS theorists believe constitute the secondary sector of the economy, are characterized by low wages, poorer working conditions, low advancement possibilities and greater employment instability. Additionally, secondary-sector workers are subject to the 'harsh and capricious work discipline' which characterized the personal relations of the labor process during the competitive era (Edwards, Reich and Gordon, 1975, p. 20); Wallace and Kalleberg, 1981, p. 88).

Segmented Labor Markets: Revised Hypothesis

The historical explanation of the evolution of segmented markets encouraged three directions in research: (1) the search for the boundaries distinguishing labor market segments; (2) analyses of the behavioral patterns of firms and individuals within each segment; and (3) the determination of the extent of mobility between segments (Reich, 1984, p. 63). The results of this search spurned a second generation of segmentation theories and caused a revision of the initial hypothesis on segmented labor markets. In contrast to the initial hypothesis, which views segmentation as the outcome of the transition from a competitive to an oligopolistic industrial structure, this new approach identifies three major institutional changes in the American political economy. Stage one, called the period of 'initial proletarianization,' began in the 1820s, became consolidated in the mid-1840s and decayed between the 1870s and 1890s. The second stage is the period of 'homogenization.' It began in the 1870s, was consolidated in the 1890s and decayed between the world wars. Segmentation is considered the third stage, which began after the First World War, was consolidated around the Second World War and began decaying in the early 1970s and continues to the present (Gordon, Edwards and Reich, 1982, pp. 2-3; Reich, 1984, p. 66). Each new stage represents the resolution of an economic crisis and the emergence of a new set of institutional structures which allow for a new period of economic growth. In considering this scenario, the character and consequences of segmentation are the same, but the timing has been changed to correspond to secular changes in economic activity, along with their accompanying labor conflicts.

During the 'initial proletarianization' a wage labor force was created out of previously independent producers. However, there was still considerable variation in the manner and extent to which employers organized and controlled the work process. Some owners 'directly supervised the organization of work while others left such direction to the workers' (Gordon, Edwards and Reich, 1982, p. 3). Although the system of wage labor grew to prominence in this era, it did not fundamentally change the organization of work.

During the subsequent 'homogenization' period, the organization of work and labor market structures were drastically changed. This primarily took the form of the reduction of skilled jobs to a common semi-skilled level with a corresponding strict control by foremen over the labor process. Machine pacing was used to drive workers. Finally, the labor market became more and more competitive.

The segmentation period which began in the 1920s was initiated by large corporations' search for more effective and reliable mechanisms of labor control. In the mid-1930s this provoked revolts among mass-production workers on an unprecedented scale, ultimately leading to the recognition of industrial unions. The segmentation process, then, is the outcome of the resolution of this unrest. It ended in accords granting union recognition, grievance procedures and seniority rights in return for employers' control over the organization of work. As a result, large corporations were able to adopt 'structured internal systems of labor management' (Gordon, Edwards and Reich, 1982, p. 16).

These developments introduced an organization of work characterized by three distinct categories of jobs. Two of these categories are in the primary sector, while a third corresponds to the unstructured processes of small firms in the secondary sector. In the primary sector a difference is made between more independent work and more subordinate work, and the corresponding sectors are referred to respectively as the independent primary sector and the subordinate primary sector. These exist alongside the secondary sector.

Boundaries of the Segmented Market

Most segmentation theorists agree that the economy is characterized by two distinct labor markets: a primary segment and a secondary segment; and by three different sectors: an independent primary sector, a subordinate primary sector and a secondary sector. But this is the limit of general agreement, since there is considerable debate over factors that determine the boundaries of these sectors and segments.

According to some authors, the distinguishing feature between segments is the presence or absence of internal labor markets. This is Doeringer's argument. But Edwards (1979) rejects this notion and suggests instead a definition based upon the structure of control within the firm. On the other hand, Althauser and Kalleberg (1981) differ from both by offering a topology of five distinct labor markets.

Other authors believe that segments are based on a cluster of personal and job-related attributes such as labor turnover and tenure, wages and fringe benefits. Still others maintain that boundaries are determined by firm characteristics such as size, profitability, market concentration and capital intensity. Some base boundaries on factors such as the presence or absence of unions, the nature and extent of workers' control over the labor process and the level of workers' autonomy. Lastly, there are those who believe that segments are bounded by racial and gender characteristics.

This ambiguity in distinguishing boundaries, a task so fundamental to the credibility of the theory, has led to criticisms and great disenchantment with the segmentation approach – even among authors sympathetic to the view. Althauser and Kalleberg maintain that the theory's poor specification has left it in disarray. Specifically, by confounding features related to the economic organization of firms with characteristics of the labor force and labor market, alongside those of demographic groups, the theory's

106

corroboration and further development have been undermined. Additionally, ambiguity stems from the assumption that segmented markets overlap nearly perfectly with ethnic and gender distinctions. That is, primary-sector firms employ prime-age white males, while secondary sector firms hire minority workers (Althauser and Kalleberg, 1981, p. 120). Later, we attempt to unravel this confusion. But first we consider the characteristics of the three sectors according to the manner in which they are most commonly perceived.

The Primary Sector

Since most segmentation theories have as their point of departure the topology initially proposed by Doeringer and Piore (1971) and reformulated by Piore (1975), we will use this as a point of reference. The initial thesis proposed a dual labor market consisting of a homogeneous primary segment and a secondary segment. Later it was reformulated in such a way that the primary segment was subdivided into an independent primary sector and a subordinate primary sector. These upper and lower tiers of the primary segment are referred to as the core of the economy. In the core,

> employers possess a high degree of market power, have at least part of their sales guaranteed by government contracts, and are usually able to generate sufficient profits to be able to pay nonpoverty wages . . . Their profitability permits them to invest in both physical and human capital, which in turn increases the productivity of labor . . . The magnitude of the wage level induces workers to value these jobs, while the high fixed costs associated with the aforementioned investments encourage employers to value stable job attachment by their workers.
>
> (Harrison and Sum, 1979, p. 689)

Although the primary market benefits from demand stimulated by government contracts, the capital-intensive nature of this sector causes the level of employment generation to be modest.

The upper tier of the primary segment, the 'independent primary sector,' is composed of professional and managerial jobs which are distinguished from the lower tier by higher pay, greater status

107

and promotional opportunities. They are also characterized by greater job turnover and mobility of labor, similar to that of the secondary sector. However, unlike the latter, turnover in this tier is voluntary and rewarded, because it is associated with occupational advancement. Jobs are distinguished by the absence of the elaborate work rules and administrative procedures that characterize the lower tier. Finally, there is an internalized 'code of behavior,' and a greater formal educational requirement.

Jobs in this tier place a premium on creativity, problem-solving, initiative and high professional standards, and they offer greater economic security. In short, this tier allows more job control and provides large returns to formal education and personal job-related attributes.

Formal education, craft union membership, or licensing is an essential requisite for employment in the upper tier, and workers identify closely with their occupations (Edwards, 1979, p. 177). There is a great deal of job security, established career patterns of advancement and relatively high pay. Finally, they differ from subordinate primary jobs by typically requiring general, rather than firm-specific, skills. According to Edwards, three groups of jobs dominate the independent primary market. The first fills the middle layers of the firm's employment structure and consists of jobs for long-term clerical, sales and technical staff, foremen, bookkeepers, personal and specialized secretaries, supervisors and so on. A second group of independent primary jobs grows out of craft work that employs electricians, carpenters, plumbers, steamfitters and machinists. A third large group of independent primary jobs includes the professional positions: accountants, research scientists, engineers, registered nurses and doctors, lawyers and tax specialists and others. As the jobs in these three groups indicate, the independent primary market, like the other segments, spans both blue-collar and white-collar work (1979, p. 174). Edwards indicates also that state employment is very important in this sector, accounting for about a fifth to a third of its total employment and for 35 percent to 45 percent of professional and technical employment.

By contrast, work in the lower tier of the primary segment, the 'subordinate primary sector,' is more routinized. These subordinate primary-sector jobs correspond mainly to well-paid unionized blue-collar occupations (Harrison and Sum, 1979, p. 689; Piore,

1975). As such, even though they are routinized, they still require dependability, discipline and acceptance of the firm's goals.

Subordinate primary-sector jobs still provide well-defined paths of advancement. Workers receive positive returns to schooling, particularly high school and slightly beyond, but experience a great deal of cyclical unemployment. Yet, even when unemployed, such workers maintain a close connection to and identify strongly with their jobs. The presence of unions is common though not a necessary feature of this sector. Occupations included are auto assembly, steelmaking, electrical products manufacturing, metal fabrication and the like. Also included are unionized workers in lower-level sales, administration and clerical jobs and transit-related occupations such as railroad engineers, interurban and transit-system bus drivers and airline maintenance personnel. Finally, workers in retailing, wholesaling and the utilities are considered part of the subordinate primary sector (Edwards, 1979, p. 171).

Using a different method than is used in the literature reviewed thus far, we have identified the occupations belonging to the primary sector – see Table 4.1. The method of deriving this classification is discussed in the later sections of this chapter. We should note at this point that while 60.56 percent of white workers hold primary-sector jobs according to this classification, only 44.51 percent of blacks do.

The Secondary Sector

Jobs in the secondary sector tend to have lower wages and fringe benefits, poor working conditions, high labor turnover, poorer chance of advancement and often arbitrary and capricious supervision. According to Doeringer and Piore (1971), the behavior of workers in this sector corresponds to the character of the sector's jobs, and vice versa. As such, workers exhibit greater turnover, higher rates of lateness and absenteeism.

There is a great similarity in this variation of segmentation theory and the approach of the conservative school. The difference is that Doeringer and Piore attribute this behavior to cultural and sociological deficiencies among workers as well as to the negative feedback associated with job characteristics in the secondary sector.

Table 4.1 Primary-Sector Occupations

Census occupation classification
(A) Managerial and professional specialty
Executive, administrative and managerial
Officials and administrative, public admin.
Other executive, admin. and managerial
Management related
Professional specialty
Engineers
Math and computer scientists
Natural Scientists
Health diagnosing
Health assessment and treatment
Teachers, college and university
Teachers, excluding college and university
Lawyers and judges
Other professional specialty
(B) Technical, sales and administrative support
Technicians and related
Health technologists
Engineering and science technicians
Other technicians
Sales
Sales representative, finance and business
Sales representative, commodities (except retail)
Sales related
Administrative support, including clerical
Supervisors
Computer equipment operators
Secretaries, stenographers, typists
Financial records processing
Other administrative, including clerical
(C) Service
Protective service
Other service
Health
(D) Precision production, craft and repair
Mechanics
Construction
Other production, craft and repair
(E) Farming, forestry and fishing
Forestry and fishing

According to Harrison and Sum, the secondary labor market is characterized by a class of employers 'whose labor intensive technologies and lack of market power restrict their ability (and their need) to pay high wages' (1979, p. 690). These low wages and fringe benefits, along with the undesirable working conditions, discourage or inhibit stable job attachment, the lack of which then impedes unionization.

> Low fixed costs, attributable especially to low rates of human capital investment in the form of specific training, induce a similar lack of concern for stability on the part of employers. These jobs therefore display low pay and high turnover. The unstable product demand causes an unstable year-round demand for labor. The sector is characterized by a good deal of seasonal employment and relatively lower productivity.
>
> (Harrison and Sum, 1979, p. 690)

Another salient feature of this sector is repetitiveness of the production processes. This means that tasks are easily learned by unskilled workers. Further, few skills are acquired while on the job, and virtually anyone can enter secondary jobs. In fact, young workers typically begin their careers in the secondary sector. The problem however is that many adults are 'unable to escape from it and spend much of their lives there' (Harrison and Sum, 1979, p. 690). Edwards likewise describes this sector as one where jobs are low-paying, unstable and dead-end, and where workers encounter frequent periods of lay-offs and are rewarded little for seniority. Further, employees lack any rights and are treated 'simply as a commodity unfettered and unencumbered by any job structure, union, or other institutional constraints' (Edwards, 1979, p. 167).

Finally, because such jobs tend to be self-terminating and unattractive, they provide little incentive for workers to stick to them, and this leads to a high voluntary labor turnover. Hence, unemployment in the secondary sector is not associated with workers waiting to regain an accustomed position, but is part of a shuttling process from one low-paying position to another.

Edwards details the jobs in this segment as consisting of low-skill occupations in small nonunion manufacturing firms, janitors, waiters and waitresses, hospital orderlies, delivery men, attendants, guards, personal care and other workers in services, lower positions in retail and wholesale trades such as sales and stock clerks, and lower-level clerical jobs such as filing, typing, key-punching and other such positions. Finally, also included are migrant and seasonal workers (Edwards, 1979, p. 167).

Despite the emphasis on a negative feedback which generates incompatible worker characteristics, we still reject this thesis both because it is an inaccurate description of most workers in the secondary sector and because it fails particularly to explain why blacks are disproportionately concentrated in secondary jobs.

We will shortly demonstrate the flaws in this description of secondary workers using relevant data. But Chapter 3 has already given an indication of our approach in this respect. There it was shown, even after controlling for significant job-related attributes, that blacks were 20 percent more likely to hold secondary-sector jobs than were whites (see Table 3.13). The identification of occupations in this segment using our criterion (which will be discussed momentarily) is given in Table 4.2. According to this classification, 55.49 percent of blacks are secondary workers, while only 39 percent of whites are.

Race, Class and Boundaries in Segmented Markets

Just as social scientists experience difficulty in identifying boundaries of social classes, we have seen that analogous problems occur with regard to identifying the boundaries of segmented labor markets. This problem is particularly acute once race and/or class is introduced.

According to Schervish, blacks, unskilled white males and women are generally tracked to secondary-sector jobs. This tracking is facilitated by mobility barriers (1983, p. 21) and reinforced by residence, inadequate skills, poor work histories and discrimination (Doeringer and Piore, 1971, p. 166). Some analysts believe that segments coincide with ethnicity, while others assert that sub-markets for minority workers exist within each segment (Gordon, Edwards and Reich, 1982, p. 360). The segment is then bounded by some job-specific or personal attribute of which blacks are believed to possess a greater or lesser quantity, such as high labor turnover.

On the other hand, Edwards offers an altogether different criterion for distinguishing boundaries. Labor market segments,

Table 4.2 Secondary-Sector Occupations

Census occupation classification

(A) Sales
Supervisors and proprietors
Sales worker, retail and personal

(B) Administrative support
Mail and message distributors

(C) Service
Private household
Other service
Food
Cleaning and building

(D) Operators, fabricators and laborer
Machine operators, assembly, laborers
Machine operators and tenders, except precision
Fabricators, assemblers
Inspectors and samplers
Transport and material moving
Motor vehicle operators
Other transport and material moving
Handlers, equipment cleaners, helpers and laborers
Construction laborers
Freight, stock and material handlers
Other handlers, equipment cleaners, helpers
and laborers

(E) Farming, forestry and fishing
Farm operators and managers
Farm workers and related

---

according to him, express the 'system of control inside the firm' (1979, p. 178). The secondary sector corresponds to simple control, the subordinate primary sector to mixed technical and union control, and the independent primary sector to bureaucratic control. These levels of control in turn dictate the degree of skill and training required of workers in the sector.

Descriptions of boundaries become even cloudier when attempts are made to introduce class. Piore comes closest to our approach by noting that the characteristics of the upper tier, lower tier and secondary sector suggest the distinctions between the middle-class, working-class and lower-class subcultures (1975, p. 127). However, he does not sufficiently specify these classes or 'class subcultures.' On the other hand, Edwards's description is specific, but its sociological accuracy is more questionable. In his approach fractions of the working class correspond to labor market segments. Fraction one, the working poor, lives in poverty primarily because the principal wage earner is in the secondary labor market and thereby experiences immobility, discrimination and low wages. Included are blacks, Hispanics, females, teenagers and undocumented workers. But the problem here is that ethnic and gender characteristics are used to constitute class categories. Fraction two consists of the traditional proletariat and is equivalent to the subordinate primary sector. Finally, fraction three is the 'middle layer' and corresponds to the independent primary sector. This is the preserve of white male workers (Edwards, 1979, pp. 185-7).

The typical explanation by LMS economists of the position of blacks in segmented markets is that blacks moved into the wage labor market during the monopoly stage when internal labor markets and its resulting segmentation were consolidated. The internal market then restricted black mobility. But our historical examination in Chapter 2 illustrates that blacks were in the skilled trades long before the evolution of monopolies and were driven out by racial animosities and discriminatory laws. This means that racial conflict and political strife, rather than the evolution of internal markets, are the most crucial ingredients in the secondary status of black labor.

This account contrasts also with the one given by Gordon, Edwards and Reich (1982). They contend that the current pattern for blacks crystallized after the Second World War as they migrated out of the South. This led to the development of a labor surplus in the North, causing blacks to be concentrated in the secondary sector. As residential segregation increased, manufacturing jobs became suburbanized and the housing stock deteriorated, blacks became trapped in central cities where they constituted a significant proportion of the low-wage labor supply to peripheral industries. But even in core industries blacks were still segregated. During the 1960s three developments took place. (1) Protests and prosperity opened opportunities in core industries for blacks. (2) Blacks gained access to the independent primary sector. And (3) expansion of welfare 'provided an alternative to low wage employment for many blacks in the reserve army of labor.' This latter development forced employers to search for new sources of excess labor, causing them to turn to Puerto Ricans, Chicanos and others (1982, pp. 206-9).

Our historical account differs by locating the origin of segmented markets for blacks in the antebellum labor strife which drove them out of skilled trades into low-wage menial occupations. This was further accelerated by the overthrow of Reconstruction and the long period of Jim Crow segregation. But in a more real sense, one can say that the segmentation of black labor began with the institution of African slavery in America.

The Conservatism of LMS Theory

Dual labor market theorists have proposed a 'signaling model' which supposedly explains the negative feedback between discrimination in labor markets and black investment in education, training and other job-related attributes. The argument is that prejudice leads blacks to invest less in schooling and other labor-enhancing activities and thereby develop fewer characteristics conducive to strong labor market performance. These traits, it is believed, are reinforced by so-called negative characteristics associated with lower-class subcultures. Hence, the lower earnings of blacks are a consequence of their poorly developed job attributes.

Barrera (1979, pp. 174-84) does an excellent job of classifying and criticizing these feedback theories. According to his scheme, this particular theory cuts across two classifications: the 'cultural/social structure deficiency theory' and the 'biased theory.' These approaches combine explanations of racial prejudice and discrimination with a deficiency component emanating from 'ghetto pathologies.' The 'pathologies' are produced by discrimination, and both phenomena are considered to be mutually reinforcing.

The recognition of a feedback effect in the production of so-called 'pathologies' distinguishes dual labor market models from conservative models. The latter believe that deficiencies in labor supply originate within the culture and social structure of black society, and reject a major causal link to discrimination. Alternatively, dual labor market economists recognize and emphasize the extent to which segmented markets negatively impact workers trapped in the secondary sector. This feedback mechanism is discussed by Ryan (1981) in a rather explicit attempt to identify two types of segmentation: that which exists before entering the labor market (pre-market segmentation) and that which occurs while actively in the labor market (in-market segmentation). Pre-market segmentation, he maintains, is closely related to social stratification. As such, individuals will bring to the market capabilities in terms of knowledge, skills and attitudes that are largely shaped by class, status, race and sex. In-market segmentation is reflected by the differences in employment opportunities or job rewards, salaries and opportunities for training – even where individuals have equally productive capabilities (1981, p. 5). The author indicates that there may be a strong interaction between these two types of segmentation because positive in-market prospects may positively influence pre-market preparations and development of labor quality and vice versa (1981, p. 10).

Although LMS theory highlights the reciprocal influence of secondary jobs on work habits, as opposed to simply blaming poor habits on workers, the theory is often too ambiguous on the causal direction of this feedback. For example, one is almost as likely to find statements in the LMS literature claiming that bad workers create the need for secondary labor markets as one is to encounter the opposite position, that bad jobs create bad work habits. But the very notion that most secondary workers display bad work habits is erroneous. This, along with the inability to identify the boundaries of secondary markets and the place of ethnic minorities within them, stands as the most significant of the theory's weaknesses. Consider the following observation by Doeringer and Piore:

> The central problem in changing the work force is that the secondary sector is the product of an interaction between workers and jobs. Jobs are adjusted by management to the traits of the labor force hired to perform them. But, at the same time, the characteristics of the work environment develop habits of behavior and thought among the work force. Thus, if secondary workers are placed in primary jobs, they may gradually learn to attend regularly, show up on time, accept prohibitions on pilferage, utilize institutionalized channels for expressing grievances, and acquire the skills necessary to care for equipment.
>
> (1971, pp. 178–9)

Apart from the inference that secondary workers have poor work habits, this statement is ambiguous on the fundamental causes of such habits. One of the most popular views of secondary workers is that they display high degrees of labor turnover. In fact, some authors suggest that the extent of labor turnover is the major difference between segments – and constitutes their boundaries. But others have acknowledged that secondary-sector workers have long job tenures.

By contrast, Harrison places the blame squarely on the character of the job itself.

> The frequently heard argument that the major barrier excluding the poor from employment is their own lack of motivation to work ignores an important strand in labor market segmentation theory: Motivation, in particular, and worker behavior, in general, are formed in response to confinement. In acclimatizing themselves to local work arrangements, some workers may find it psychologically as well as technically difficult to move from one stratum to another. Embedded in the dual labor market is the hypothesis that productivity and stability increase as wages increase. Thus, at low wages prevalent in the secondary segment, poor productivity and lack of motivation are to be expected.
>
> (Harrison and Sum, 1979, p. 693)

In Edwards's assessment the instability of workers' job performance is a consequence of the organization of their jobs (Edwards, Reich and Gordon, 1975, p. 13). But to Piore, the adverse behavior of secondary workers is rooted in lower-class family neighborhoods, schools and subculture, and this lower-class subculture is itself the carry-over into adulthood of adolescence behavior. This behavior, he maintains, is distinguished by the absence of family formation, lack of stabilization in employment patterns and absence of a transition in the character of peer-group activities (1975, p. 145).

The close similarity between this aspect of LMS theory and propositions of conservative economists is striking. Therefore, in the closing sections of this chapter, we will examine empirically the association between race, segmentation and worker characteristics.

Segmentation and Discrimination

The purpose of this section is to examine the extent of segmentation in contemporary labor markets. In particular, we address the following questions. First, can a theoretically acceptable criterion be developed to segment labor markets? Second, assuming the first task is accomplished satisfactorily, we would like to know how blacks and whites are distributed across segments and the extent to which race is a factor in this distribution. Third, what are the characteristics associated with workers across segments, and do these correspond to the hypotheses already mentioned on segmentation? Finally, what is the extent of mobility between segments? These questions are addressed below.

Recall that in LMS literature there does not exist an agreed criterion, either empirically or theoretically, for segmenting the market. Techniques have varied widely but may generally be classified as those segmenting by: (1) firm/industry characteristics, (2) occupations, (3) job characteristics, (4) individual/human capital characteristics and (5) some combination of these. Even the most popular approach, which uses firm/industry characteristics to segment markets, has been shown to be incapable of unambiguously classifying firms or industries in either the primary or the secondary sector. Additionally, serious problems are encountered when one attempts to correlate firm/industry characteristics with class categories.

Approaches employing individual attribute or human capital characteristics have encountered problems of a different nature, commonly referred to as truncation bias (Cain, 1976, pp. 1240-1). Schervish describes this very concisely. 'If sectors are divided in the first place on the basis of income level, then estimated coefficients of the impact, say, of education on earnings are biased' (1983, p. 26). Using low income to define the secondary sector truncates the dependent variable and biases the impact of additional education on earnings towards zero, at least in the simple regression model. This may give the false appearance that there is no reward for increased education in the secondary sector while there is in the primary sector. And since LMS economists have always been preoccupied with proving that returns to productivity differ by segments, this finding (which is based on biased regression models) has been an important ingredient of their argument.[3]

What we desire is a method for identifying labor market segments that (1) can be made consistent with our approach to class stratification and (2) avoids the problem of truncation bias. The most efficient way to accomplish this is to base segments on occupational categories. Reich (1984) and Gordon, Edwards and Reich (1982) employ a combination of criteria to allocate occupations to three segments. These criteria are based on levels of educational development and vocational preparation corresponding to jobs listed in the *Dictionary of Occupational Titles* (US Employment Service, 1973-6 [1965]). Factor analysis and personal judgement are then used to categorize each three-digit occupation (Reich, 1984, pp. 80-1).

Our approach views the labor market as being segmented fundamentally by occupational characteristics. The challenge then is to identify occupational segments in a way that is intuitively appealing and operational. You may recall that Tables 4.1 and 4.2 listed the occupations of the primary and secondary sectors, without giving an explanation of the basis for the derivation. That scheme is derived from our attempt to distinguish two classes of labor: *general labor* and *specific labor*. These concepts are adopted from Becker's notion of specific training and general training. By specific training Becker refers to an investment which enhances a worker's 'human capital' in such a way that the increase in the worker's productivity accruing to one firm is specific to that firm and not transferable to others. On the other hand, the increase in productivity of a worker receiving general training can be experienced not only by the worker's current firm but by any firm employing the worker (see Doeringer and Piore, 1971, pp. 13-16, citing Becker, 1964).

This is an extremely useful starting point because it allows one to associate individual worker attributes with job characteristics. The one revision we make is to define specificity in terms of its transferability not among firms but rather among occupations. In particular, we say that labor is general if a worker can transfer from one occupation to another (whether within or across firms) without an adverse impact upon the firm's productivity. On the other hand, the occupational transfer of specific labor, unaccompanied by additional education or training, adversely impacts productivity. *Our approach then defines the primary sector by specific labor and the secondary sector by general labor.*

This method does not assume that all workers having general labor are low-income, low-skill workers. For example, an administrator as well as a dishwasher may possess general labor if both are capable of moving from one occupation to a different occupation without any additional training or adverse impact on firm productivity. This of course differs from Doeringer and Piore's observation on general labor. They maintain that 'generally transferable skills are approximated by basic literacy, by the ability to communicate, and by a commitment to industrial work rules' (1971, p. 16).

It is important to point out this difference, because if all general labor is low-educated, low-income and low-skill labor, then segmenting labor markets by this criterion would be equivalent to truncating the dependent variable and introducing bias in regression analysis. But our method avoids the problem of truncation bias.

Secondly, because we do not bound labor market segments by firm or industrial-sector characteristics, the question of how segments have arisen in response to the changing structure of the economy does not take on primary importance. In fact, our perspective is that segmented markets have always existed regardless of the stage of economic development. The more interesting point is what is the character of the segments at each stage of development, who occupies them during any given time, how do returns to labor productivity differ between segments, and what is the extent of inter-segmental labor mobility? In general, these questions are very similar to the ones we addressed in analyzing social classes; and we would like our method to assist in correlating segmented labor markets with segments of social classes. But if we bound segments by firms or industries, this would be impossible, because social classes or internal class segments do not correspond to firm or industry characteristics.

The focus on occupational characteristics does not mean that we are uninterested in the evolutionary structure of firms and industries. We are interested to the extent that such changes alter the production relations and occupational structure, and thereby change the character of segmented labor markets.

One crucial objective in identifying market segments is to test the hypothesis that individuals in the secondary sector are not rewarded on the basis of productivity as is the case for workers in the primary sector. In fact, the existence of a difference across segments in economic returns to productivity and job-related attributes is critical in many interpretations and has often constituted the axis around which the credibility of the theory revolves. Unfortunately, we will not address this question empirically but will establish an unambiguous criterion for dividing the labor market into segments. Thereby a basis is provided for examining returns to productivity at a later date. Secondly, we do not employ our criterion to distinguish an independent primary sector from a subordinate primary sector, but focus only on the primary and secondary segments.

Given the class stratification we derived earlier, an independent primary sector is akin to our concept of the new middle class. Earlier we defined this class segment by the extent to which it possesses scarce forms of human capital. Therefore, to make these two concepts consistent, we would have to drop from the independent primary sector those workers not possessing such unique skills. On the other hand, occupations commonly associated with the subordinate primary sector constitute the primary segment of the black working class. Workers in this class segment also possess specific skills but these skills are not scarce enough to allow their possessor to command extraordinarily high wages. Along with subordinate primary-sector workers, secondary-sector workers are also part of the working class; recall from Chapter 2 that we divided this class into primary, secondary and marginalized segments.

For simplicity we concentrate on identifying two labor market segments: the primary sector and the secondary sector. As indicated, primary workers are distinguished by specific labor, while secondary-sector workers are identified by general labor. In order to make this idea practical, we use the information contained in the *Current Population Survey* supplemental tapes, 'Occupational Mobility, Training and Job Tenure,' January 1983. The relevant question of this survey asks: 'Did you need specific skills or training to obtain your current (last) job?' The range of responses are 'yes' and 'no.' We cross-tabulated the responses by 44 two-digit occupations based on the 1980 Census of Population Occupation Classification System. If, for each occupation, the majority of workers (50.1 percent or greater) responded yes, this occupation was classified in the primary sector. Otherwise, it was placed in the secondary sector. Actually there was little ambiguity in classification, since outcomes for almost all occupations were overwhelmingly either yes or no. Tables 4.3 and 4.4 record the results and the corresponding segmentation scheme. Beside each occupation is the percent of respondents answering yes to the specific skills requirement question. The resulting segmentation scheme is intuitively appealing. Additionally, it is very simple but at the same time avoids the problems of ambiguity and truncation bias discussed earlier.[4]

According to Tables 4.3 and 4.4, managerial and professional specialty occupations are classified in the primary sector along with most technical, sales and administrative support occupations. Among sales occupations, supervisors and proprietors are classified in the secondary sector. In fact, this category has the highest percentage (47.8 percent) of respondents answering yes to the specific skills question of any secondary-sector occupations. While technical, sales and administrative support occupations generally fall within the primary sector, service workers, operators, fabricators and laborers are classified as secondary-sector occupations.

Table 4.5 employs the segmentation scheme developed above to classify black and white workers. As expected, a disproportionate percentage of black workers hold secondary-sector jobs, 55.49 percent as compared to 39.44 percent for whites.

One question immediately comes to mind. That is, to what extent are these disproportions created by demographic and human capital factors as opposed to purely racial factors? If we examine the geographic distribution of workers by race and segment (see Table 4.6) we find two facts. First, the South accounts for a greater percentage of secondary workers than any other region; 64 percent of black secondary workers reside in the South while 31.0 percent of white workers do. Second, a higher percentage of blacks who work in the South are secondary workers (61.3 percent) than is the case in any other region. For whites, the highest percentage of secondary workers is to be found in the North Central (42.7 percent). Without further examination, this gives the distinct impression that geographic living preferences, and not race, are a primary factor in the segmentation of the labor force.

To examine this, we conducted a logit analysis of the characteristics associated with the probability of holding a primary- and a secondary-sector job – see Table 4.7. The dependent variable is the logarithm of the odds of holding a primary-sector job, and the independent variables are the job-related attributes of workers

Table 4.3 Primary Occupations and Skill Requirement

Census occupation classification	Per cent needing specific skills or training for current job
(A) Managerial and professional specialty	
Executive, administrative and managerial	
Officials and administrative, public admin.	64.9%
Other executive, admin. and managerial	68.4
Management related	68.3
Professional specialty	
Engineers	91.9
Math and computer scientists	90.7
Natural scientists	100.0
Health diagnosing	100.0
Health assessment and treatment	94.8
Teachers, college and university	96.4
Teachers, excluding college and university	93.9
Lawyers and judges	86.9
Other professional specialty	87.6
(B) Technical, sales and administrative support	
Technicians and related	
Health technologists	78.9
Engineering and science technicians	74.6
Other technicians	92.4
Sales	
Sales representative, finance and business	66.8
Sales representative, commodities (except retail)	57.2
Sales related	51.8
Administrative support, including clerical	
Supervisors	79.7
Computer equipment operators	75.7
Secretaries, stenographers, typists	71.7
Financial records processing	64.9
Other administrative, including clerical	53.3
(C) Service	
Protective service	61.1
Other service	
Health	60.5
(D) Precision production, craft and repair	
Mechanics	56.9
Construction	55.5
Other production, craft and repair	55.2
(E) Farming, forestry and fishing	
Forestry and fishing	55.5

Table 4.4 Secondary Occupations and Skill Requirement

Census occupation classification	Percent needing specific skills or training for current job
(A) Sales	
Supervisors and proprietors	47.8%
Sales worker, retail and personal	27.4
(B) Administrative support	
Mail and message distributors	21.1
(C) Service	
Private household	9.7
Other service	
Food	30.8
Cleaning and building	15.4
(D) Operators, fabricators and laborer	
Machine operators, assembly, laborers	
Machine operators and tenders, except precision	31.2
Fabricators, assemblers	
Inspectors and samplers	38.5
Transport and material moving	
Motor vehicle operators	38.5
Other transport and material moving	41.5
Handlers, equipment cleaners, helpers and laborers	
Construction laborers	14.4
Freight, stock and material handlers	22.8
Other handlers, equipment cleaners, helpers and laborers	16.3
(E) Farming, forestry and fishing	
Farm operators and managers	23.0
Farm workers and related	18.0

Table 4.5 Segmentation by Race, 1983

	Number	Percent of black or white
Secondary sector		
White	36,469,964	39.44
Black	5,854,884	55.49
Primary sector		
White	56,003,349	60.56
Black	4,696,349	44.51

Source: CPS microdata tapes, January 1983

Table 4.6 Distribution of Workers by Sector,
Region and Race, 1983

	Regions				
	Northeast	North Central	South	Northwest	
Secondary[a]					
White	36.3	42.7	39.8	39.1	
Black	45.2	54.4	61.3	40.7	
Primary[a]					
White	63.7	57.3	60.2	60.9	
Black	54.8	45.6	38.7	59.3	
					Total
Secondary[b]					
White	20.1	29.0	31.2	19.7	100
Black	12.9	16.1	64.0	6.4	100
Primary[b]					
White	23.1	25.6	31.1	20.2	100
Black	19.7	17.6	51.0	11.7	100

[a]Column percentages for blacks and whites.
[b]Row percentages for blacks and whites.
Source: CPS microdata tapes, January 1983.

included in the supplemental study of occupational mobility (see Table 3.13 and pages 85-7 for a fuller discussion of the technique and definition of the independent variables). For each attribute, the coefficient to standard error ratio is listed beneath the value of the coefficient. The sample population is further subdivided by sex (male and female) and ten-year age cohorts. This allows a more careful examination of sexual and age differences attributable to segmentation. The results are quite revealing.

The number of years of education completed (Highed) has a highly significant impact on the log of the probability of holding a primary-sector job, and this is true across gender and age cohorts. Second to this, however, race (as measured by Black) has a significantly negative impact on the probability of being in the primary sector. While the coefficient for race (-0.1173) is statistically insignificant for black males aged 25 to 34, it is large and significant for all other age and gender cohorts. The log of the odds of being in the primary sector for blacks aged 35 to 44 is -0.4559 lower than it is for whites,

Table 4.7 Logit Analysis Results

Variable	Male			Female	
	Age group (years)			Age group (years)	
	25–34	35–44	45–54	25–39	35–44
Black	−0.1173	−0.4559	−0.5942	−0.0208	−0.2331
	−1.3026	−4.5399	−4.5699	−2.3629	−2.2988
Age	0.1443	−0.1538	0.0950	0.1233	0.5672
	0.7007	−0.4640	0.1963	0.5304	1.5410
Agesq	−0.0022	0.0020	−0.0009	−0.0020	−0.0071
	−0.6490	0.4793	−0.1979	−0.5137	−1.5169
Ushrswh	−0.0006	−0.0011	0.0036	0.0141	0.0216
	−0.2001	−0.2777	0.7384	4.7722	5.9378
Highed	0.1835	0.1651	0.1681	0.2556	0.2527
	15.1294	12.8291	11.5658	13.9980	12.0574
Lpreempl	0.0097	0.0045	0.0068	0.0294	0.0017
	1.2974	0.8831	1.7990	2.4387	0.2251
Hlngwk	0.0262	0.0069	0.0078	0.0260	0.0153
	3.5328	1.3798	1.9968	2.8779	0.8402
Ncentrl	−0.0849	0.0661	−0.1350	−0.1319	0.0856
	−1.1354	0.7303	−1.3405	−1.4791	1.3108
South	−0.0704	0.1029	−0.0189	−0.0526	−0.1254
	0.9493	1.1626	−0.1903	−0.5845	−1.3108
West	0.0259	0.1415	−0.0434	−0.1401	−0.0718
	0.3404	1.5068	−0.4017	−1.5129	−0.6828
Intercept	0.2128	5.9323	0.4889	−0.5682	−10.0573

Note: Coefficient to standard error ratio is shown below the value.

and it is even lower for blacks aged 45 to 54 years. On the other hand, the probability for black females being in the primary sector is lower and statistically significant for both the first age cohort, 25 to 34 years, and the second cohort, 35 to 44 years.

The lack of significance for the first age cohort of males (25 to 34 years) is perhaps due to decreasing discriminatory barriers in the form of segmented labor markets confronting younger blacks. This is to be expected given the institutional changes in society. However, one must be warned to interpret this result with extreme caution.

Specifically, while the extent of in-market segmentation against young black males is obviously lower than it is for older black males, younger blacks are much more likely to be unemployed and out of the labor market. The extent to which this is a function of segmented markets is not examined here.

Of the remaining variables, the usual number of hours worked each week (Ushrswh) is, as would be expected, statistically significant for females but not for males. Although the log of the probability increases with the number of hours worked per week, the coefficients are very small, suggesting that the size of the impact is also very small. Finally, the level of job skill, as measured by the length of time a person has worked in his or her present occupation (Hlngwk), is statistically significant for the youngest cohort, but again the size of the coefficient is small. Significance in all respects is measured at the 0.05 level.

We have therefore provided conclusive evidence to answer the question above. Our conclusion is that *race is a very significant factor in the allocation of workers across labor market segments. More directly, blacks have a lower probability of holding primary-sector jobs and a higher probability of holding secondary-sector jobs than do whites — other things being equal.*

The average age of workers by segments is given in Table 4.8, which indicates that blacks in the secondary sector are slightly older than whites, while in the primary sector they are roughly 2.3 years younger.

A better picture of age is given in Table 4.9, which examines age distribution of cohorts across race and segmented labor markets. Notice that (for the column percentages given at the bottom half of the figure) the concentration of young blacks in the secondary sector is very high: 77.8 percent for ages 18 to 19 years, and 61.6 percent for 20 to 24 years. This is also true for older

Table 4.8 Sectors by Mean Age of Workers, 1983

Sector	Average age	
	White	Black
Primary	38.3 years	36.0 years
Secondary	35.2	36.6

Source: CPS microdata tapes, January 1983.

Table 4.9 Age Distribution by Segmented Markets and Race, 1983

	Age						
	18–19	20–24	25–34	35–44	45–54	55–59	Total
Secondary sector[a]							
White	7.1	17.4	24.3	16.4	13.6	6.6	85.4
Black	5.9	17.1	25.5	18.8	17.2	5.5	90.0
Primary sector[a]							
White	2.0	11.9	30.9	24.2	16.6	6.8	92.4
Black	2.1	13.4	38.4	23.2	13.1	6.5	96.7
Secondary sector[b]							
White	70.0	48.9	34.0	30.8	34.9	38.8	
Black	77.8	61.6	45.6	50.5	62.3	51.7	
Primary sector[b]							
White	30.0	51.1	66.0	69.2	65.1	61.2	
Black	22.2	38.4	54.4	49.5	37.7	48.3	

[a]Row percentages.
[b]Column percentages.

Source: CPS microdata tapes, January 1983.

blacks: 62.3 percent for ages 45 to 54 years, and 51.7 percent for 55 to 59 years. On the other hand, for whites, concentration in the secondary sector is high for 18- to 19-year-old cohorts (70.0 percent), but declines to 48.9 percent for 20- to 24-year-olds, and declines even further and remains relatively low even for the oldest cohorts. This implies that, while young whites can be expected to make a significant movement out of the secondary sector with increasing age, no such change occurs for blacks (at least as revealed by cross-sectional data). This gives vivid support to the contention of LMS economists that blacks remain trapped in the secondary sector even with increasing age. But we should qualify this observation by noting that a single cross-section of data is not really the most appropriate way of capturing this essentially life-cycle phenomenon.

On the other hand, there is evidence to refute a major hypothesis of segmentation economists. Specifically, the contention is that secondary workers in general, and black workers in particular, are characterized by greater labor turnover. Some authors believe this characteristic is so typical of secondary workers that they use it as a criterion to distinguish segmented markets. But a check of actual results finds that such a hypothesis cannot be supported – see Tables 4.10 and 4.11. These tables measure the median number of years of tenure with present employer and occupational mobility rate among black and white workers. The results, based on the US Department of Labor's 1983 study of occupational mobility and tenure, indicate that blacks have a longer median tenure than whites, 3.6 years as opposed to 3.2 years.[5] Additionally, Table 4.11

Table 4.10 Length of Time on Current Job, 1981

	White		Black	
Total number	82,375,000		8,514,000	
Median years	3.2		3.6	

	White		Black	
Age groups	Men	Women	Men	Women
Total 16 years and over	4.0	2.4	4.0	3.3
16 to 24 years	0.9	0.8	0.7	0.8
25 to 34 years	2.9	2.0	3.0	2.7
25 to 44 years	6.7	3.3	6.2	5.2
45 to 54 years	11.2	5.7	10.0	8.1
55 to 64 years	14.9	9.1	14.4	10.3
65 years and over	10.1	9.8	12.0	11.9

Source: US Department of Labor (DOL), 1983.

Table 4.11 Occupational Mobility Rate[a] by Race and Sex, 1981

	Men		Women	
	All persons	Black	All persons	Black
Total, 16 years and over	10.3	9.2	12.0	8.6
20 to 24 years	23.8	25.4	22.8	18.2
25 to 34	12.4	10.9	13.9	10.8
35 to 44	7.4	4.9	8.9	7.1
45 to 54	4.4	5.0	5.8	3.7
55 to 64	3.5	3.3	2.7	0.9
65 and over	1.6	0.7	1.8	0.0

Overall occupational mobility rate: white = 11.9, black = 8.4.
[a]Percent of persons employed in both January 1981 and January 1980 who were employed in a different occupation in January 1981 than January 1980.
Source: US DOL, 1983, pp. 5, 27.

reveals that whites change occupations much more frequently than do blacks. The former's occupational mobility rate is 11.9 percent while for blacks it is 8.4 percent. These results should immediately dispel some popular myths about black workers. There may well be a small percentage of black secondary workers who are chronically mobile, but in no way can this be said to be true of most blacks.

Between January 1982 and January 1983, 7.5 million workers changed occupations. Table 4.12 disaggregates these job changers by race and labor market segment. The first figure indicates that a higher percentage of black occupational changers are in the secondary sector than is the case for whites, that is, 56.6 percent of black occupational changers as opposed to 44.0 percent of whites. Conversely, a greater percentage of white occupational changers are in the primary sector as opposed to blacks, 55.0 percent versus 43.3 percent. But consider this in the context of Table 4.5, which gives the percent distribution of blacks and whites among segments. The percentage of blacks in the secondary sector, 55.49 percent, and in the primary sector, 44.51 percent (see Table 4.5), corresponds almost identically to the distribution of black job changers by sector. That is, 56.6 percent and 43.3 percent of all black changers were in the secondary and primary sectors respectively. On the other hand, while 39.44 percent of whites are in the secondary sector, 44 percent of white job changers were secondary-sector workers. Hence, relative to their distribution across segments, a greater percentage of occupational changers in the secondary sector are white than black.

Table 4.12 Percent of Workers Changing Jobs, 1983

	Percent changing jobs between Jan. 1982 and Jan. 1983
Secondary sector	
White	44
Black	56.6
Primary sector	
White	55
Black	43.3

Source: CPS microdata tapes, January 1983.

Table 4.13 Profile of Job Changers by Age (Percent), 1983

	Age				
	18–19	20–24	25–34	35–44	45–54
Secondary sector					
White	9.1	31.0	30.2	12.5	7.0
Black	29.5	23.5	15.6	19.4	1.8
Primary sector					
White	6.0	20.2	40.2	20.7	8.1
Black	25.7	48.9	11.1	6.1	3.6

Source: CPS microdata tapes, January 1983.

Table 4.13 further profiles these changers by race, age and segment. We notice that among blacks a large percentage of job changes takes place between ages 18 to 24 in both the secondary and the primary sector, and the amount of changes for workers older than this is relatively small in comparison. For whites, changes increase significantly for ages 20 to 34. The interesting point is that for young blacks (ages 18 to 24 years) the percent changing occupations is more than three times that of young whites. But the percent of prime-age working blacks (20 to 34 years) changing occupations overall is much lower than that of whites. For both black and white workers aged 18 to 24 years, the major reason given for changing occupations is the desire for better pay or full-time work. Forty-four percent of all workers in this age cohort cited this as the reason for changing. These two reasons are followed in importance by 'lost job or laid off,' which accounted for 15.2 percent. Furthermore, across all age brackets the search for better pay accounts for a slightly larger percentage of black occupational changers than white changers (US DOL, 1983, p. 6). We recognize that a change in occupation is not the same as a change in job and the LSM thesis of a high labor turnover of secondary sector workers is based on frequent job changes. Yet the extent of occupational changes does give a picture of the fluidity of workers, particularly in the secondary sector because that sector is characterized by the absence of specific skill requirements across occupations.

131

Table 4.14 Inter–Sectoral Mobility of Job Changers, 1983

Part I: All job changers

1983	1982 Secondary sector	Primary sector
Secondary sector	63.2[a]	36.8
	62.0[b]	31.1
Primary sector	32.2[a]	67.8
	38.0[b]	68.9

Part II: White job changers

1983	1982 Secondary sector	Primary sector
Secondary sector	63.1[a]	36.9
	60.9[b]	30.6
Primary sector	32.5[a]	67.5
	39.1[b]	69.4

Part III: Black job changers

1983	1982 Secondary sector	Primary sector
Secondary sector	64.6[a]	35.4
	76.2[b]	38.6
Primary sector	26.4[a]	73.6
	23.6[b]	61.4

[a]Row percent.
[b]Column percent.
N = 7,551,840.

Finally, we would like to know the extent of inter-sectoral mobility and the degree to which this varies by race. Table 4.14 addresses this issue. Part I of the table indicates that among all individuals changing occupations between January 1982 and January 1983 (i.e. 7,551,840) and holding a secondary sector job in 1982, 62.0 percent changed to new occupations in the secondary sector while 38.0 percent changed to new occupations in the primary sector. Among whites the comparable percentages were 60.9 percent and 39.1 percent, while among blacks the respective percentages were 76.2 percent and 23.6 percent. Hence, there was a sixteen–percentage–point difference between whites and blacks moving from the secondary to the primary sector. Although we have not examined the job related attributes associated with this differential in occupational mobility, based on our analysis of such attributes thus far, one would be safe in assuming that there also exists racial inequities in this process.

Conclusion

We have seen that one of the most fundamental ways in which discrimination exists today is in the form of differentials in access to certain occupations. When the labor force is segmented and a primary and secondary sector are identified, it is found that blacks are disproportionately concentrated among secondary-sector occupations, and this is so even after having controlled for job-related attributes, age and other demographic differences. Thus to understand the full dimensions of labor market discrimination one must also examine inequalities emanating from segmented labor markets along with wage discrimination, which was discussed in Chapter 3. Yet even these do not provide a complete understanding. This is because we have thus far limited our study to employed workers. But blacks constitute a disproportionate share of the unemployed and discouraged labor force. Hence, the dynamics impacting their earnings and occupational distribution also impact their disproportionate representation among the unemployed.

Notes: Chapter 4

1 A second thrust within the neoclassical paradigm centered on 'perceptual discrimination' – Arrow, 1972a, 1972b; Phelps, 1972. But this approach, which seeks to explain the existence of income inequalities and labor queues, is completely different from the segmentation and dual labor market approaches – which seek to

explain why two completely different market clearing mechanisms exist for labor.

2　See Barrera, 1979, for a good explanation and critique of these theories.

3　Schervish, 1983, p. 26, cites a list of major studies that commit this error.

4　When a more formal clustering procedure is used for the same purpose, the only difference is that 'supervisors and proprietors' is grouped in the private sector.

5　We should point out that the results refer to the median tenure as a specific date and not the expected tenure over one's lifetime.

5 *Conservative Economics:* False Prophecies, Failed Policies

To get a grip on the problems of poverty, one should also forget the idea of overcoming inequality by redistribution. Inequality may even grow at first as poverty declines. To lift the incomes of the poor, it will be necessary to increase the rates of investment, which in turn will tend to enlarge the wealth if not the consumption, of the rich.

(Gilder, *Wealth and Poverty*, 1981, p. 67)

'Trickle down' economics, as reflected in the above quotation, constitutes the essence of conservative approaches to the elimination of poverty and inequality. Sparked by the capture of the White House in 1980, the supply-side revolution has since galloped towards failure. The depths of its demise are reflected in the fact that today few economists or policy-makers will identify with the theory. Not only have all major supply-siders fled Washington; more traditional supply-side economists have gone to great lengths to distance themselves from the economic chaos left behind. As Martin Feldstein recently asserted, in a discussion of supply-side economics it is important to 'distinguish the traditional supply-side emphasis that characterized most economic policy analysis during the past 200 years from the new supply-side rhetoric that came to the fore as the decade began' (1986, p. 26).

No one would deny that conservatives inherited an economy seriously weakened by escalating inflation. But when a doctor operates on a patient with a serious illness, he can cure the illness and save the patient, or kill the patient to cure the illness. The White

House boasts of having cured inflation are reminiscent of a doctor who has chosen the latter approach. Inflation has been cured, but in the process the economy was brought to its knees by a deep recession, enormous budget deficits and record trade imbalances.

It is ironic but not surprising that supply-side policies, whose tax cuts were supposed to generate additional revenues or at least be self-financing, have caused a $220 billion deficit. Rather than stimulating the supply-side of the economy, these policies caused a rapid dislocation of the economy's supply base, making heavy industry no longer competitive internationally and driving agricultural producers into bankruptcy in record numbers. A theory whose acclaimed tax cuts were to generate new productive investment, long-run capital formation and accelerated job growth has produced only record mergers and acquisitions. Finally improvements in employment have been experienced, but only after the economy traversed the deepest recession and highest unemployment levels in postwar history. The growth that we have experienced has resulted mainly from an excessive and ill conceived mix of fiscal policies in the areas of tax cuts, military expenditures and deficit financing.

Gilder's Multifarious Metaphysics

A good part of the contemporary supply-side vision can be attributed to George Gilder: not because he is the theory's formulator,[1] but because his *Wealth and Poverty* (1981) provided the 'long awaited' grand ideological synthesis to the disparate trends in neoconservative thought (Kinsley, 1981, p. 25).

Until the Great Depression, economic thinking was dominated by the classical theory embodied in Say's Law, developed by J. B. Say and James Mills. In short, the law states that the very process of production and aggregate supply generates an amount of income to the factors of production, via wages, rent, profits and interest, that is equal to the value of the commodities produced. Assuming all income is spent and not hoarded or saved, total spending (demand) will be equivalent to total production. If a portion is saved, an equivalent amount will be invested, so long as interest rates are flexible. Likewise, it was believed that flexible prices in the product market and flexible wages in the labor market would ensure full employment at market clearing prices. Taken together, these propositions led Say to conclude that 'supply creates its own demand.' Keleher and Orzechowski have observed:

> Say's Law indicates that it is production and aggregate supply rather than demand and expenditure that create growth and wealth, the tax (and expenditure) policies in harmony with the law are those which foster aggregate supply (rather than aggregate demand). If taxes adversely affect aggregate supply or factor inputs, for example, supporters of Say's Law indicate that these taxes should be either eliminated or minimized.
>
> (1981, p. 27)

But the collapse of investment during the Great Depression – even while interest rates were below 2 percent and there was persistent excess supply despite low commodity prices and 25 percent unemployment even at low wages – led to the abandonment of classical economics and the emergence of the Keynesian revolution.

For the first time orthodox economists were forced to recognize that, left to market forces, the capitalist system had no inherent proclivity towards full employment prosperity as predicted by Say. Stagnation therefore called for government intervention through stimulative policies. So Keynesian demand management policies emerged to dominate the economic landscape in the post-war era. But by the mid-1970s these policies were falling into disfavor.

The inability to contain inflation, declining productivity, creeping unemployment and stagnating output set the stage for the supply-side revolution. Citing the failure of Keynesian policies of the late 1960s and 1970s, supply-siders rejected all attempts by the government to achieve full employment stabilization through demand-oriented fiscal and monetary policies. Instead, they blamed such policies as being responsible for stagflation.

Keynesianism, the supply-siders maintained, was also responsible for a general decline in the economics profession as best epitomized by the failure of economists to predict economic behavior reasonably and consistently using rigorous econometric models.[2] The major shortcoming of such models was seen as their failure to account for the impact of incentives on investment, innovation, and growth. Accordingly, only supply-side policies emphasized this aspect. Gilder put it this way:

> reversion to the supply-side means leaving the comforts of rigorous models and computations and again entering the fray of history and psychology, business and technology. Economists should again focus on the multifarious mysteries of human social behavior and creativity which Adam Smith luminously addressed in *The Wealth of Nations*, which Marx stuffed into the maw of his theory, which Keynes treated in most of his writings, and which even Galbraith, in his often perverse way, delights in describing.
>
> (1981, p. 40)

According to supply-siders, the most fundamental issue to understand is the nature, role and determinants of incentives in the economic system. The basic premise is that fiscal policy, and in particular taxes, has a major impact on incentives. We were told that taxes determine not only the supply of labor, savings and capital to the productive process, but ultimately the long-run growth of the economy and government revenues. Since decisions regarding the supply of productive factors are made at the margin, the relevant tax is not total or average taxes, but the marginal rate of taxes. That is, the increased tax liability accompanying an increase in income.

According to Keleher (1981, pp. 19, 20), a reduction in marginal tax rates would affect at least four factors:

1 The price of leisure vis-a-vis work. Leisure becomes more expensive in terms of forgone income, thereby encouraging a greater willingness to work.
2 The price of current consumption relative to future consumption, i.e. savings and investment. The opportunity cost of current consumption becomes more expensive because of the increased return on savings and investment. Therefore, the latter increases.
3 The return to work in the market economy vis-a-vis work in the nonmarket (underground) economy. In short, lower taxes make individuals more likely to declare earned income for tax purposes.

4 The return on taxable investment increases, causing an increase in capital formation and a decrease in nonproductive tax-sheltered investment.

Tax reductions, by altering relative prices, were supposed to generate a shift towards greater production, employment and output. But not only this; Laffer and Conley (1978) claimed that low marginal taxes would be so stimulative that they would ultimately increase government revenue, totally offsetting their cost. In short, supply-side economists believed that a reduction in marginal taxes would increase economic growth, employment and government revenue.

The first assumption, that the supply of labor would increase due to a reduction in taxes on labor income, was (even at the time it was conjectured) the most empirically tested and consistently invalidated aspect of their propositions. Reduced taxes were supposed to bring about increases in the cost of leisure relative to work and thereby positively influence work attitudes, reduce absenteeism rates and encourage a willingness to accept overtime. Along with the increase in labor supply, tax revenues were supposed to increase because of the greater willingness of workers to leave the underground (nontaxed) economy.

Secondly, lower marginal taxes, we were told, would positively influence savings. This contrasts with the Keynesian dynamic where tax reductions increase disposable income and aggregate consumer spending. Supply-siders assumed that increases in savings would overwhelm consumption increases for two reasons. First, the opportunity cost of consumption would increase because of the greater rate of return on savings. Second, the greatest tax benefit would accrue to the upper income bracket, whose marginal propensity to save is greater than that of the lower income bracket.

The fact that supply-side tax cuts were initially designed to channel a disproportionate share of income to the wealthy was not apologized for, but rather central to the logic of the theory's proponents. According to George Gilder, greed is characteristic of the lower classes, while 'giving' (that is, investment) is fundamental to the capitalist class. Any attempt to achieve an egalitarian society through taxing the rich will only promote 'greed over giving.' Besides, he proclaims, 'all material progress is ineluctably elitist'

(1981, pp. 30, 259). And so supply-side policies proceeded with a passionate belief in 'trickle down' economics.

Finally, it was hypothesized that lower marginal taxes would positively impact investment behavior through greater profit expectations. Once enacted, these changes would so stimulate savings, investment, output, productivity and employment, that the tax revenue accruing from the generation of new income would more than offset the loss of government revenues due to tax cuts.

The failures of these policies are by now too well known to merit much reiteration. Epstein (1986) has compiled key indices of economic performance, measured from business cycle peak to cycle peak from 1949 to 1985. His results, reproduced in Table 5.1, indicate that over the first five years of supply-side policies economic performance was worse in every relevant category except inflation.

Epstein states that these indicators reveal 'continuing economic deterioration under conservative economics.' And when asked how much it costs to reduce inflation by one point, he answers: $200 billion (1986, p. 42).

More relevant to our topic of inequality is Gilder's ideological vision. The kernel of his contribution to this conservative phenomenon was his attempt to provide a moral defense of free market policies – uninhibited by a need to empathize with those at the bottom of the economic ladder. To Gilder, the most important

Table 5.1 Economic Indicators, Business Cycle Averages, 1949–85 (Percentages)

	Unemployment rate	Real GNP rate	Change in real wages	Net exports/ GNP ratio	Productivity growth	Inflation rate
1949-53	4.1	5.0	4.0	0.9	3.7	2.2
1954-6	4.7	2.5	3.5	0.8	2.2	0.5
1957-9	5.5	2.5	2.7	0.8	3.0	2.4
1960-9	4.8	4.2	2.8	0.7	2.9	2.3
1970-3	5.3	3.7	2.1	-0.1	2.9	4.9
1974-9	6.8	2.8	0.3	-0.8	0.8	8.6
1980-5	8.1	2.1	-0.005	-1.9	1.3	6.7

First three quarters of 1985.

Source: Epstein, 1986, p. 42.

event in recent history is the demise of the socialist dream, and the second most important event is the 'failure of capitalism to win a corresponding triumph' (1981, p. 3). Hence, he charges all conservatives with the primary responsibility of defending with passion the historic and moral victory of free market capitalism and denying the 'robber baron' myth of its founding. Kristol responds: 'such good cheer in defending capitalism we have not seen since Malthus and Ricardo transmuted Adam Smith's basic optimism into a "dismal science"' (1981, p. 414). In *Capital*, Marx proclaimed:

> The discovery of gold and silver in America, the extirpation, enslavement and entombment in mines of the aboriginal population, the beginning of the conquest and looting of the East Indies, the turning of Africa into a warren for the commercial hunting of black-skins, signalized the rosy dawn of the era of capitalist production.
>
> (1967, p. 751)

But Gilder counters with the belief that 'capitalism begins with giving' (1981, p. 21). And far from being based on greed, it is based on generosity. To Marx, the motive force of investment was a greed for profits and the force of competition. To Keynes, it was animal spirits. But to Gilder, it is the 'rewards of giving.' In a classic but typical example of Gilder's metaphysics, he asserts:

> Capitalist production entails faith in one's neighbors, in one's society, and in the compensatory logic of the cosmos. Search and you shall find, give and you will be given unto, supply creates its own demand.
>   . . . The gifts of advanced capitalism in a monetary economy are called investments. One does not make gifts without some sense, possibly unconscious, that one will be rewarded, whether in this world or the next. Even the biblical injunction affirms that the giver will be given unto.
>
> (1981, pp. 24-5)

Giving, risks, innovation and faith in the cosmos are fundamental to success. Because the wealthy are the givers, any attempt to achieve an egalitarian society through taxing the rich will only promote 'greed over giving.' Naturally, to Gilder such greed is characteristic of the lower classes. In fact, he cites two reasons why one should be less concerned with egalitarianism. First, all progress is elitist, and secondly, wealth and poverty are less a state of income than a state of mind (1981, pp. 12, 105, 259).

Irving Kristol felt compelled to comment that Gilder provides a 'pseudo-anthropological analysis of economic activity: and that a market economy may provide growth, but it certainly cannot offer us consolation amidst disaster' (Kristol, 1981, p. 414). David Kaplan (1981, p. 51) indicates that 'Even those sympathetic to Gilder's sentiments might find his logic a bit shaky: having asserted, rather than demonstrated, a link between giving and capitalism, he views any instance of giving as, virtually by definition, an instance of capitalism.' Best of all, Kinsley states: 'this kind of reasoning does more to make altruism look bad than to make capitalism look good' (1981, p. 25).

Despite Gilder's multifarious metaphysics, the policy implication of such thinking is clear, and the difference in emphasis is crucial. While Keynesian demand management policies have emphasized historically the need to ensure a reasonable standard of living for the economically disinherited, supply-side economists proclaimed that greater justice is achieved through unfettered free markets. This is the real menace of *Wealth and Poverty*: that is, the amount of suffering Gilder and other supply-siders are willing to inflict upon the poor in the name of helping the poor. In the long run, they proclaim, supply-side economics will triumph. In the long run, Keynes rightly observed, we will all be dead. But if Gilder has his way, at least the wealthy will survive.

Employment Problems and Economic Status

In earlier chapters we demonstrated the existence of wage discrimination and showed also the impact of occupational discrimination on the types of jobs and occupational mobility experienced by blacks. While we will not examine empirically the link between discrimination and unemployment, it is safe to assume that, just as race adversely affects wages and occupational status, it also affects the likelihood of being employed in the first place. Employment in turn has a bearing on income, and the latter obviously impacts one's poverty status. Under the present conservative administration, all these indices of economic well-being have deteriorated for both the black and the white populations.

In the final quarter of 1986 median weekly earnings of the nation's 78.8 million full-time wage and salary workers were $368 and varied substantially by race, gender and occupation. Table 5.2 highlights the difference in earnings across race and occupation. It also reveals the adverse occupational distribution of black workers. While they are underrepresented in the relatively high-earning managerial and professional specialty occupations, blacks are overrepresented in low-paying occupations such as services and operators, fabricators and laborers. As we have

Table 5.2 Median Weekly Earnings of Full-time Workers
by Race and Occupation

	Median weekly earnings	Percent of whites employed	Percent of blacks employed
Managerial and professional specialty	505	24.9	18.0
Executive, administrative and managerial	511	9.8	6.7
Professional specialty	500	15.1	11.3
Technical, sales and administrative support	320	46.3	36.9
Technicians and related support	416	3.2	3.1
Sales occupations	351	13.1	8.4
Administrative support, including clerical	300	30.0	25.4
Service occupations	223	16.9	28.1
Private household	121	1.6	4.7
Protective service	392	0.4	0.7
Service, except private household and protective	209	14.9	22.8
Precision production, craft and repair	408	2.2	2.6
Operators, fabricators and laborers	301	8.6	14.1
Machine operators, assemblers and inspectors	293	6.2	10.6
Transportation and material moving occupations	366	0.9	1.1
Handlers, equipment cleaners, helpers and laborers	263	1.5	2.4
Farming, forestry and fishing	217	1.1	0.2
Employed, 16 years and over	368	1.0	1.0

Source: US DOL *News*, 4 February 1987; US DOL, *Employment and Earnings*, February 1986.

shown, this distribution is related to the persistence of racial discrimination in contemporary labor markets; and, although we have not said that without discrimination black and white workers would have identical occupational distributions, it is apparent that discrimination significantly impacts the present distribution.

Data on median family income in real dollars (see Table 5.3) indicate an accelerated decline during the present conservative administration which took office in 1980. In fact in 1982 the ratio of black to white income reached a low level of 55.3 percent. Further, in 1984 real median income of whites was $27,690 which represented a 3.3 percent increase over the previous year and for blacks it was $15,430 which showed no statistically significant change from 1983 (US Department of Commerce, 1985; note also that the 1984 data are derived from a different series). The 'trickle down' prediction of supply-side theorists has operated in the reverse direction for blacks. Accompanying the decline in real income, Table 5.4 illustrates the increase in poverty status of both the black and white populations. The long secular decline in the percent of people living in poverty reversed itself after 1980.

Table 5.3 Median Family Income by Race, 1970–83
(1983 Dollars)

	Black	White	Total	Black income as percentage of white income
1970	$16,111	$26,263	$25,317	61.3
1971	15,843	26,253	25,301	60.3
1972	16,347	27,504	26,473	59.4
1973	16,297	28,237	27,017	57.7
1974	16,175	27,088	26,066	59.7
1975	16,251	26,412	25,395	61.5
1976	16,175	27,192	26,179	59.5
1977	15,722	27,522	26,320	57.1
1978	16,614	28,050	26,938	59.2
1979	15,886	28,054	26,885	56.6
1980	15,324	26,484	25,418	57.9
1981	14,532	25,792	24,525	56.3
1982	14,035	25,394	24,187	55.3
1983	14,506	25,757	24,580	56.3

Source: Children's Defense Fund, 1985, table 12.

Table 5.4 Poverty Rates for Persons by Race, 1959–83

	Black	White	Total
1959	58.10%	18.10%	22.40%
1960	—	17.8	22.2
1961	—	17.4	21.9
1962	—	16.4	21.0
1963	—	15.3	19.5
1964	—	14.9	19.0
1965	—	13.3	17.3
1966	41.8	11.3	14.7
1967	39.3	11.0	14.2
1968	34.7	10.0	12.8
1969	32.2	9.5	12.1
1970	33.5	9.9	12.6
1971	32.5	9.9	12.5
1972	33.3	9.0	11.9
1973	31.4	8.4	11.1
1974	30.3	8.6	11.2
1975	31.3	9.7	12.3
1976	31.1	9.1	11.8
1977	31.3	8.9	11.6
1978	30.6	8.7	11.4
1979	31.0	9.0	11.7
1980	32.5	10.2	13.0
1981	34.2	11.1	14.0
1982	35.6	12.0	15.0
1983	35.7	12.1	15.2
1984	33.8	11.5	14.4

Source: Children's Defense Fund, 1985, table 13.

Conservatives are quick to blame these worsening income and poverty statistics on increases in female-headed families among blacks. But the facts do not provide strong support to the argument that recent declines in black/white median income and increases in poverty rates are due to this factor. Without a doubt there has been an alarming and distressing increase in female-headed families among blacks since the 1960s as illustrated in Figure 5.1. Yet over this period the poverty status of black persons showed a slight secular improvement until the 1980s. Obviously, had the collapse in stable black families not occurred the secular improvement in black poverty status would have been much greater; especially since poverty rates are greatest among female-headed families.

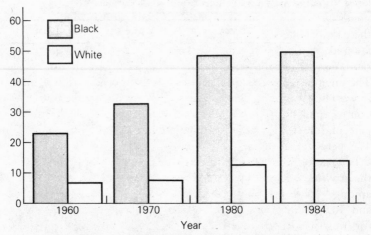

Figure 5.1 Percentage of children living in
female-headed households.
Source: Children's Defense Fund, 1985, Table 1.5.

However to place the blame upon this factor totally is erroneous.
Yet the median income of black families has continued to decline,
and their poverty has worsened.

The low income and high poverty rates of the population are
closely related to a deteriorating employment status. During 1983,
14.9 million people had to work part-time on an involuntary basis
(that is, either because their hours were reduced or because there
was no full-time work available). The median weekly earnings
for part-time workers were $99 in the fourth quarter of 1986 (US
DOL *News*, 4 February 1987). Further, 19 percent of involuntary
part-time workers are from families living in poverty. Additionally, 4.5 million full-time year-round workers had total earnings
below $6,700 – the amount of earnings an individual would have
received for 40 hours' work per week, at 50 weeks of work during
the year, at the minimum wage of $3.35 per hour. One-third of
these individuals lived in families whose earnings were below the
poverty line (US DOL, 1985). Clearly, the worsening income
status of workers is related to their declining employment status.

One of the most startling labor force developments over the last
four decades has been the widening gap between blacks and whites
in rates of unemployment, employment to population ratio and

labor force participation rate. This has been particularly true for youth workers, ages 16 to 19 years. While there was rough parity in these ratios following the Second World War, and some ratios even favored blacks, by January of 1986 the employment/population ratio was 61.5 percent for whites and 54.1 percent for blacks. The unemployment rate for whites was 5.7 percent and for blacks it was 14.4 percent. These same ratios for the white and black youth populations (16 to 19 years) were 47.8 percent versus 24.4 percent for employment to population and 14.9 percent versus 41.9 percent for unemployment rates.

Few labor force problems have received more attention than the growing unemployment and declining labor force participation among young and black workers. Bowers (1979), Cogan (1982) and Rees (1986) cite most of the popular explanations given for this secular trend. These include the following. (1) The labor market has become crowded by youth of the baby boom generation, creating an excess supply. (2) Greater supply has also been induced by increased opportunities. (3) Lower wages and segmented markets adversely influence blacks, causing them to quit jobs more frequently and conduct job searches for longer periods. (4) Increasing school attendance has made youth less committed to full-time work and more casual in their job-search behavior. (5) Suburbanization of jobs has caused a spatial mismatch and adversely affected black central city residents. (6) The increase in female labor force participation has created an excess supply. (7) The existence of minimum wage laws has priced young and black workers out of the market. (8) School enrollment causes youth employment to be more seasonal. (9) Youth have a greater turnover due to more frequent lay-offs, discharges for cause and voluntary quits. (10) Welfare has adversely influenced labor force participation. (11) Since the imposition of Fair Employment laws, employers engage more in hiring discrimination as opposed to wage discrimination. And (12) the decline in agricultural-related jobs has displaced a disproportionate number of Southern blacks. Of all factors mentioned, conservatives claim that minimum wages have the greatest impact on black unemployment.

Minimum wages, it is hypothesized, have several major affects. They price less productive young people out of the job market, lead to greater unemployment and less employment growth, and restrict the opportunity for young people to gain on-the-job training

(Bowers, 1979). As such, the abolition of the minimum wages law has become a central focus of the conservative agenda. In addition to perpetuating the large differential in black/white unemployment, they believe that this law embodies the evils of intervening in free market operations. In the next section, therefore, we turn our attention to the impact of minimum wages on black unemployment.

Black Unemployment: the Minimum Wage Excuse

To be sure, the decline in black youth employment has been dramatic. In 1955 the employment/population ratio for male blacks and whites aged 18 to 19 was 0.66 and 0.64 respectively. By 1984 these respective ratios were 0.33 and 0.60 (Rees, 1986, p. 616). Additionally, Bowers notes a reversal in black/white female labor force participation rates. After lagging for many years, white female labor force participation rates now exceed those of black females (Bowers 1979, 16).

In general, little clear explanation is provided for the extent of black youth joblessness. But to Sowell, the reason is obvious. Furthermore, he rejects any attempt to attribute this unemployment to discrimination. In his opinion, the notion that high unemployment rates among black teenagers are caused by discrimination overlooks certain historical facts. First, he points out that racial differences in teenage unemployment are of relatively 'recent vintage,' and employer discrimination was greater in the past than now. Second, the rapid rise and spreading coverage of minimum wages since the 1940s have been a dominant pattern in recent decades (Sowell, 1977, p. 4). Reviewing the evidence, he concludes that minimum wage laws cause 'substantial unemployment.'

In reality, few areas of labor market dynamics have been investigated so completely and drawn such diverse conclusions. Still, no study has found more than a minimal impact on employment. Opinions are split, but even for those believing that minimum wages adversely impact employment, the extent is thought to be relatively small. Rees's recent comprehensive review of empirical studies concludes that the impact of minimum wages 'has been greatly overemphasized' (1986, p. 620).

Brown, Gilroy and Kohen (1982) conducted one of the first reviews of the empirical findings on minimum wages. They conclude that the impact upon employment and unemployment is such that a '10 percent increase in the minimum wage is estimated to result in about a 1-3 percent reduction in total teenage employment' (1982, p. 505). The estimated impact on unemployment is less clear but varies from minus one to zero percent.[3]

Unlike these more guarded opinions, conservatives insist that minimum wages have a powerful negative impact on employment. According to Williams, two groups are affected most: youth, because of their low-skills, age and lack of work experience; and racial minorities, who are placed disproportionately among the low skilled due to discrimination. 'These workers are not only made unemployable by the minimum wage, but their opportunities to upgrade their skills through on-the-job training are also severely limited' (1982b, p. 35). He also accuses minimum wage legislation of fostering discrimination by lowering the opportunity cost of preferential hiring.

The minimum wage went into effect in 1938 and has been raised fifteen times since. The last change was in January 1981. After adjusting for inflation it has only doubled in value and is worth no more today than its 1963 value – see Table 5.5 (Singer, 1981). That is, where the minimum wage in real 1938 dollars (i.e. actual purchasing power) was 57 cents in 1963, after adjusting for inflation, it was the same in 1981 even though in nominal terms it was $3.35. Clearly, this indicates that its real wage effect on unemployment has been minimal. In 1981, 10.6 million people were employed at or below the minimum wage. Of these, 63 percent were women and 30 percent were 16 to 19 years of age. The law currently applies to 73.4 percent of all jobs in the private sector, while exemptions are given for administrative, executive and professional positions, small farms and small retail and service firms. In fact, some 500,000 young people are employed at 85 percent of the minimum wage in colleges, retail and services establishments (Singer, 1981a, p. 146).

According to Levitan and Belous (1979, p. 17), respectable studies on the impact of minimum wages 'have come down on all sides of the issue.' There tentative findings are: (1) Minimum wages have not been a major contributor to unemployment. (2) Econometric studies of the postwar period indicate that significant youth unemployment would have occurred even without the minimum wage. (3) If wages and prices are rigid, then minimum wages have a smaller impact on employment – and rigid wages

149

Table 5.5 Minimum Wages, Real and Nominal Dollars, 1938-81

	Minimum wage	Value 1938 dollars
1938	0.25	0.25
1939	0.30	0.30
1945	0.40	0.31
1950	0.75	0.45
1956	1.00	0.52
1961	1.15	0.54
1963	1.25	0.57
1967	1.40	0.60
1968	1.60	0.66
1974	2.00	0.58
1975	2.10	0.57
1976	2.30	0.58
1978	2.65	0.59
1979	2.90	0.59
1980	3.10	0.56
1981	3.35	0.57

Source: Singer, 1981a, p. 146.

are more characteristic of today's economy. (4) The social costs of minimum wages are more than compensated for by their social benefits. (5) Because changes in the minimum wage have been very modest, the positive and negative effects have been minimal. (6) Income gains due to minimum wage increases appear to be much greater then the negative employment effects. And (7) while the minimum wage does not vastly alter the income distribution pattern, it does significantly reduce poverty (Levitan and Belous, 1979). They conclude:

> In the real world, which is far different from economic models based upon perfect competition, some form of minimum wage regulation is required even from the point of allocative efficiency – not to mention equity. Equally important is the need to encourage workers to rise above the poverty threshold without relying upon income supplements . . . The minimum wage is, therefore, needed as a floor to express the socially recognized value of labor, rather than just to meet income needs.
>
> (1979, p. 19)

It appears that conservatives have vastly overemphasized the disemployment effects of minimum wages. The latter do impact employment, but as an explanation for the huge secular increase in black unemployment they fall far short. Brown, Gilroy and Kohen observe:

> While it is often asserted that blacks are more adversely affected than whites by minimum wage, previous studies provide conflicting evidence on this issue. In any case, while these studies do not disprove the claim that nonwhites are more adversely affected, we conclude from the body of literature that such an assertion must rest on theoretical rather than empirical grounds, at least insofar as the timeseries evidence is concerned.
> (Brown, Gilroy and Kohen, 1982, p. 508)

Rees concludes that the source of the decline in black employment is poorly understood. Noting that the earnings ratio between black and white workers improved while employment ratios worsened, he suggests the possibility that 'the decline in wage discrimination encouraged greater discrimination in employment' (1986, p. 615). Although we do not attribute the large unemployment differential between blacks and whites solely to discrimination, it appears that the latter must figure prominently in any realistic explanation. By comparison, minimum wages would be much less important.

In summary, conservative accomplishments have fallen far short of their prophecies. In almost every area except inflation, there has occurred an erosion in the relative state of the economy and in the well-being of blacks in particular. Yet conservatives continue to blame their failed policies on market impediments. Minimum wages are blamed for unemployment, government social programs are blamed for poverty, and Congress is blamed for the budget deficit. Fortunately, too much time has lapsed for them to continue to blame past administrations for the current state of the economy.

Few people are surprised by these failures. Even Martin Feldstein, a traditional supply-sider, has concluded:

> the new supply siders were much more extravagant in their claims. They projected rapid growth, dramatic increases in

151

tax revenues, a sharp rise in saving, and a relatively painless reduction in inflation. The height of the supply-side hyperbole was the 'Laffer curve' proposition that the tax cut would actually increase tax revenue because it would unleash an enormously depressed supply of effort.

. . . I have no doubt that the loose talk of the supply-side extremists gave fundamentally good policies a bad name and led to quantitative mistakes that not only contributed to subsequent budget deficits, but also made it more difficult to modify policy when those deficits became apparent.

(1986, pp. 27–8)

Indeed, false prophecies do lead to failed policies.

'Cast Down your Buckets': Conservatives on Civil Rights

Booker T. Washington's famous Atlanta Exposition speech of 1895 implored blacks to cease political agitation for racial equality and cast down their buckets. With this, he became a symbol of the acceptance of the status quo, and blacks vehemently opposed him. True enough, Washington's aim was to promote black economic advancement. But faced with intransigent racial oppression, he denied having any interest in social equality, he pledged loyalty to a 'beloved New South' that politically and economically disenfranchised blacks through the judicial system, social caste and lynch mobs and he even denounced Reconstruction (Meir, 1968, p. 339).

In many respects, today's black conservatives are inheritors of this conciliatory spirit. But one crucial difference is that Washington had a large audience within the black community because of his strong institutional ties to black social development. Most of today's black conservatives castigate black leadership and denounce civil rights organizations from institutional affiliations totally alien to mainstream black life. Little wonder they are greeted with such fierce hostility and have almost no significant black following.

Conservatives claim that black leaders and organizations are totally bankrupted. Furthermore, they claim that racism is not the cause of the economic and social distress within black society. But most incredibly, they contend that political activity and political success are neither necessary nor sufficient for economic advancement (Sowell, 1984, p. 32). In fact, Sowell asserts, 'it would perhaps be easier to find an inverse correlation between political activity and economic success than a direct correlation' (1984, p. 30). His proof for this assertion consists of a cursory examination of successful ethnic minorities that have avoided political involvement in their quest for economic advancement – for example, the Jews and the Chinese. But this method is insufficient to support the claim.

First, Sowell's list of ethnic groups is not a random sample but a biased sample of success stories. As such, it does not include groups that have shunned political activity and still remained economically and politically oppressed. It might be claimed that Sowell's purpose is simply to show that politics is neither necessary nor sufficient for advancement, and therefore one or several success stories are sufficient. But this is not the case, because he uses these exceptions to establish a general rule.

To assert that an inverse relationship exists between economic advancement and political involvement is a generalization that can only be based on examining a representative sample. Furthermore, even if we accept the contention that these groups have not been involved in politics, the importance of such an assertion is negligible because Sowell has not controlled for any other relevant sociopolitical factors that may have influenced their attitudes towards political involvement. By failing to do the latter, one cannot refute the assertion that an apolitical ethnic group that has advanced economically would have progressed even further had it engaged in politics. Nor can one refute the assertion that politically involved ethnic groups that have not advanced economically would have been worse off had they not engaged in politics. For example, it is ludicrous to maintain that blacks would be better off economically and socially had they not engaged in the Civil Rights Movement.

Cross-cultural comparisons such as Sowell undertakes (1984, pp. 29-35) prove little and violate a principle that is fundamental even to conservative criticisms. That is, sufficient factors must be controlled to adequately compare different outcomes across ethnic groups.

Conservative economics has had a profound adverse effect upon national economic policies, programs and strategies designed to assist and promote black economic advancement; and black conservatives have assumed a vanguard role in this regard.[4] There are two aspects to their offensive. First, they advocate a free market approach to the problems plaguing black society. For example, abolition of the minimum wage or establishment of a sub-minimum wage along with the removal of government regulations is viewed as a way to eradicate black unemployment. Second, their most vociferous attack has been upon traditional civil rights organizations, their agendas and leadership. Affirmative action, they maintain, has set black economic advancement back, and traditional civil rights leaders and organizations are misleading the black masses. Harry M. Singleton asserts: 'Traditional civil rights groups are proponents of bankrupt policies that have outlived their usefulness and are no longer valid or workable' (Singer, 1981, p. 435).

In Sowell's opinion, the battle for civil rights was fought and won 'two decades ago,' and the succeeding years have confirmed that denial of civil rights cannot explain the extent of racial and social problems.

> In reality, the historic data show that (1) the economic rise of minorities *preceded* passage of the Civil Rights Act of 1964 by many years, (2) the existing upward trend was *not* accelerated, either by that Act or by quotas that became generally mandatory in 1971, and (3) during the era of affirmative action, such disadvantaged blacks as young males with little experience or education, and members of female-headed households, actually *retrogressed* relative to whites of the same description, while more advantaged blacks rose both absolutely and relative to their white counterparts. In short, although affirmative action invokes the name of the disadvantaged, these are precisely the people who have fallen behind under its auspices.
>
> (1984, pp. 133-4)

In Sowell's opinion, the setback caused by affirmative action is evident by the fact that in 1969, before the establishment of numerical goals, black family income as a percent of whites' was 62 percent. By 1977 it fell to 60 percent. Secondly, he asserts that the number of blacks in professional, technical and other high-level occupations doubled during the decade prior to the passage of the Civil Rights Act in 1964. In short, occupational gains were greater during the 1940s and 1950s when there was no civil rights legislation (1984, p. 84). Because he is intent on denying that any positive contribution is made by political involvement, Sowell goes to great lengths to demonstrate that little or no progress has resulted from the civil rights struggle. The facts, he maintains, do not support the civil rights vision. Further, it was not antidiscrimination laws that made the difference, but the fact that blacks acquired literacy, higher levels of education, greater skills and increased cultural exposure. 'The advancement of blacks was not simply a matter of whites letting down barriers' (Sowell, 1984, p. 84).

These are indeed curious observations on Mr Sowell's part. In the first place, it is erroneous to date the changes brought on by the Civil Rights Movement to the passage of the Civil Rights Act in 1964. The dynamics of this movement began long before the Act was passed, and its roots can be traced back to the 1940s.

The Civil Rights Movement of the 1950s and 1960s and the Black Power Movement of the late 1960s and 1970s initiated profound changes both on the demand side of the economy and on the supply side. Civil rights victories were accompanied by an unparalleled opening of educational opportunities, and by new opportunities in the labor market. It makes little sense to attempt to divorce the improvements in the quality of black labor and other supply-side changes from the civil rights struggle that made them possible. Sowell's contention that changes were more rapid in the 1940s and 1950s before civil rights activities overlooks the fact that civil rights struggles existed then as well. The March On Washington Movement (MOWM), initiated and financed by A. Philip Randolph's Brotherhood of Sleeping Car Porters, organized over 100,000 blacks for a march on Washington in 1941 to protest employment segregation. This threatened action forced President Roosevelt to issue an executive order banning discrimination in defense industries and establishing the Fair Employment Practices Committee (FEPC) (Foner, 1981, pp. 238-44). Furthermore, it was the Brotherhood, led by E. D. Nixon, the Montgomery President, that organized the successful bus boycott which sparked the modern Civil Rights Movement. Change did not simply begin with the passage of an Act in 1964. Civil rights laws have grown out of their corresponding political movements and usually postdate the latter, sometimes by many years. To assess the impact of the movement by narrowly focusing upon the law, as Sowell does, is erroneous. Taken out of historical context, the Civil Rights Act means little. But within its proper context it is possible to witness the profound changes this struggle has brought about. Sowell asks: 'Why should discussions of positive achievements by blacks ever be a source of embarrassment, much less resentment, on the part of black leaders? Because many of these positive achievements occurred in ways that completely undermine the civil rights vision' (1984, p. 84). By this he means that progress was much greater before the Civil Rights Act. But it is Sowell who attempts to deny progress to fit his vision. Black leaders do not resent or deny progress. What they have asserted is that progress has not been broadly based. This much they share in common with conservatives. But the latter also reject all social programs because they claim that these have benefited only the black middle class.

What such critiques fail to recognize is that the new black middle class evolved largely out of civil rights victories and is a new phenomenon. Many blacks, currently occupying this station, are only one decade removed from poverty or very humble roots.

A profile of five prominent black conservatives should suffice to prove this point. Singer's (1981b) interview with these gentlemen indicates that each had a very humble origin and has achieved noteworthy success as part of the new black middle class. It is instructive to look at their backgrounds and relative attainment, because these are the very individuals who are quick to accuse social action programs of having benefited only the *existing black elite*.

Sowell indicates that his parents were 'low skilled' and lived in a house without running water until he was 9. He was a high-school dropout, factory worker and Marine recruit until he attended Harvard College and the University of Chicago. Walter Williams, J. A. Parker and Robert Woodson were all products of broken homes and were raised in the slums of Philadelphia. Harry Singleton's father was a janitor, his mother a factory worker. All these individuals received advanced degrees at distinguished institutions and currently occupy prominent professional positions (Singer, 1981b). Their success may or may not have been favorably impacted by social changes created by the Civil Rights Movement. This is not the issue. The point is that their backgrounds and advancement have not been dissimilar at all to those of most blacks of their generation who have since become part of the new black middle class.

When conservatives accuse programs such as affirmative action of benefiting only a privileged few, it is as if they believe that only the black elite has benefited, when in fact the new black middle class evolved during this era and has roots, just as these conservatives do, only one decade removed from the black poor and working class. But for the opportunities opened in society through the civil rights struggle, most members of the new middle class would still be a part of the working class. In making this observation, we are not defending the uneven impact of social programs. This is a matter of grave concern and highlights a need to overhaul such programs to better address the needs of the disinherited. But it does not suggest that such programs need to be dismantled completely, as advocated by conservatives.

The problem that affirmative action is accused of – that is, fostering development of a black elite alongside the persistent impoverishment of the masses – is not an affirmative action problem *per se*. Instead, this dynamic is rooted in the very nature of the kind of free market system advocated by conservatives. To achieve a different outcome, there must be market intervention; but this is what conservatives abhor most. There is, then a contradiction in the logic of their argument.

Notes: Chapter 5

1 According to Gilder, 1981, the theory's primary developers are Norman Ture, Arthur Laffer, Paul Craig Roberts, Robert Mundell, Jude Wanniski, Alan Reynolds and Michael Evans. Hailstone, 1982, indicates that its major propositions are outlined in works such as Friedman and Friedman, *Free to Choose*, 1980; Gilder, *Wealth and Poverty*, 1981; Toffler, *The Third Wave*, 1980; Wanniski, *The Way the World Works*, 1978.

2 See criticisms by Gilder, 1981, p. 414; Keleher, 1981; Kristol, 1981, 1981; Supel, 1980.

3 One problem with examining unemployment is the difficulty in identifying labor force withdrawals created in response to minimum wage increases.

4 Singer, 1981b, identifies the most prominent of the black conservatives and their philosophical positions.

Conclusion: Race, Class and Conservatism in Retrospect

Today, race, class and conservatism are critical issues, and this investigation has attempted to bring them into clear focus. In doing so we found these seemingly disparate topics to be intricately connected. In fact, our initial objective, of evaluating conservative propositions on race, could not proceed until we specified the interaction between racial inequality and class stratification. Therefore Chapter 1 was devoted to an interpretation of class. We combined several approaches to derive a final synthesis which was then used to examine the contemporary nature of stratification in black society. Once accomplished, we addressed a key topic of debate: that is, the relative position of class and race in the life chances of blacks.

If class station is more important than race, then much of the inequality between ethnic groups cannot be attributed to discrimination. Rather, it is a logical consequence of differential dispersion across the class spectrum. But we demonstrated that the logical flaw in this argument is the assumption that class station among blacks, no matter how important, is determined independently of racial subordination and conflict. To the contrary, a historical and contemporary examination of the main stages of Afro-American development illustrates that racial antagonism plays a determining role in the character of black stratification. But to understand this one cannot limit one's examination to broad class categories, as most researchers do. Instead, the internal structure of classes must be examined – that is, their segments and strata.

Next we turned our attention to conservative propositions on race. Reduced to their lowest common denominator, these propositions imply that discrimination cannot account for the disadvantaged status of blacks in American society. To conservatives, numerous factors explain this better than racial discrimination. These include ethnic differences in age, education, geographical location, job experience, occupational distribution, family size and culture. Examining these separately and then collectively, we concluded that racial discrimination is still an important contributor to the relative disadvantaged status of blacks. Further, the investigation of segmented labor markets explained the most important contemporary form of labor market inequality. Not only are qualified blacks relegated disproportionately to lower-status jobs, but their concentration in such positions is reinforced by occupational mobility barriers.

The high-sounding promises of supply-side economics have not materialized, leaving key aspects of the economy in shambles and its proponents embarrassed. Nor does the current administration appear to have a solution to the problem. Freer markets have not reduced poverty but worsened it. Lower taxes have created a colossal deficit rather than a balanced budget. Finally, race relations have not improved with the dismantling of affirmative action and reversal of the Justice Department's enforcement of civil rights. Instead, they have reached their lowest ebb in decades. We can thank the conservative revolution for these grand failures.

Unable to acknowledge these facts, conservatives are galloping towards oblivion. Today there is little programmatic substance left to their once fiery agenda, which just seven short years ago swept the nation. But reality has been bitter and time unkind to conservatives. Why so? Because people cannot eat ideology, no matter how pure.

Appendix:
Geographic Divisions
of the United States

New England Division
Maine
New Hampshire
Vermont
Massachusetts
Rhode Island
Connecticut

Middle Atlantic Division
New York
New Jersey
Pennsylvania

East North Central Division
Ohio
Indiana
Illinois
Michigan
Wisconsin

West North Central Division
Minnesota
Iowa
Missouri
North Dakota
South Dakota
Nebraska
Kansas

South Atlantic Division
Delaware
Maryland
District of Columbia
Virginia

West Virginia
North Carolina
South Carolina
Georgia
Florida

East South Central Division
Kentucky
Tennessee
Alabama
Mississippi

West South Central Division
Arkansas
Louisiana
Oklahoma
Texas

Mountain Division
Montana
Idaho
Wyoming
Colorado
New Mexico
Arizona
Utah
Nevada

Pacific Division
Washington
Oregon
California
Alaska
Hawaii

References

Alexis, M., and Medoff, M. (1984), 'Becker's utility approach to discrimination: a review of the issues,' *Review of Black Political Economy*, vol. 12, no. 4, pp. 41-58.

Althauser, R., and Kalleberg, A. (1981), 'Firms, occupations, and the structure of labor markets: a conceptual analysis,' in I. Berg (ed.), *Sociological Perspectives on Labor Markets* (New York: Academic Press), pp. 119-49.

Arrow, K. (1972a), 'Models of job discrimination,' in A. Pascal (ed.), *Racial Discrimination in Economic Life* (Lexington, Mass.: D. C. Heath-Lexington Books) ch. 2, pp. 83-102.

Arrow, K. (1972b), 'Some mathematical models of race in the labor market,' in Pascal, op. cit., ch. 6, pp. 187-203.

Arrow, K. (1974), 'The theory of discrimination,' in O. Ashenfelter and A. Rees (eds.), *Discrimination in Labor Markets* (Princeton, NJ: Princeton University Press) pp. 3-33.

Barrera, M. (1979), *Race and Class in the Southwest: A Theory of Racial Inequality* (Notre Dame, New Brunswick: University of Notre Dame Press).

Bates, T. (1973), 'The potential of black capitalism,' *Public Policy*, vol. 21, no. 1, pp. 135-48.

Becker, G. (1964), *Human Capital: A Theoretical and Empirical Analysis, with Special Reference to Education* (New York: Columbia University Press).

Becker, G. (1971 [1957]), *The Economics of Discrimination* (Chicago: The University of Chicago Press).

Bell, D. (1973), *The Coming Post-Industrial Society* (New York: Basic Books).

Bell, D. (1975), *The Cultural Contradictions of Capitalism* (New York: Basic Books).

Bell, D. (1979), 'The new class: a muddled concept,' *Society*, vol. 16, no. 2, pp. 15-23.

Bergman, B. (1971), 'The effect on white incomes of discrimination in employment,' *Journal of Political Economy*, vol. 79, no. 2, pp. 294-313.

Black Enterprise (1973), June; (1983), June.

Blinder, A. (1973), 'Wage discrimination: reduced form and structural estimates,' *Journal of Human Resources*, vol. 8, no. 4, pp. 436-55.

Block, W., and Walker, M. (1982), *Discrimination, Affirmative Action, and Equal Opportunity: An Economic and Social Perspective* (Vancouver, British Columbia: Frazier Institute).

Bluestone, B. (1970), 'The tripartite economy: labor markets and the working poor,' *Poverty and Human Resources Abstracts*, vol. 5, no. 4, pp. 14-35.

Boneparth, E. (1976), 'Black businessmen and community responsibility,' *Phylon*, vol. 37, no. 1, pp. 26-43.

Boston, T. (1972), 'The problems of economic growth: a survey and analysis of Hogan's Creek,' report prepared for the City Department of Housing and Urban Development, Jacksonville, Florida.

Boston, T. (1982-3), 'Capitalist development and Afro-American land tenancy,' *Science and Society*, vol. XLVI, no. 4, pp. 445-60.

Boston, T. (1985), 'Racial inequality and class stratification: contributions to a critique of black conservatism,' *Review of Radical Political Economics*, vol. 17, no. 3, pp. 47-71.

Boston, T. (1987a), 'Distribution of earnings gains and losses in labor force migration: an exploration using CWHS data,' unpublished paper, College of Management, Georgia Institute of Technology, Atlanta.

Boston, T. (1987b), 'Mr Sowell and the economics of discrimination: a critique,' unpublished paper, College of Management, Georgia Institute of Technology, Atlanta.

Bowers, N. (1979), 'Young and marginal: an overview of youth employment,' *Monthly Labor Review*, vol. 102, no. 10, October, pp. 4-18.

Brown, C., Gilroy, C., and Kohen, A. (1982), 'The effect of the minimum wage on employment and unemployment,' *Journal of Economic Literature*, vol. 20, no. 2, pp. 487-528.

Brown, W. W. (1976 [1880]), 'My Southern home,' in D. Sterling (ed.), *The Trouble They Seen: Black People Tell the Story of Reconstruction* (Garden City, NY: Doubleday).

Burnham, J. (1941), *The Managerial Revolution: What is Happening in the World?* (New York: The John Day Company, Inc.).

Cain, G. (1976), 'The challenge of segmented labor market theory to orthodox theory,' *Journal of Economic Literature*, vol. 14, no. 4, pp. 1215-57.

Campbell, R., and Johnson, D. (1981), *Black Migration in America* (Durham, North Carolina: Duke University).

Children's Defense Fund (1985), *Black and White Children in America: Key Facts* (Washington, DC: Children's Defense Fund).

Clark, K., and Gershman, C. (1980), 'The black plight: race or class?' *New York Times Magazine*, 5 October, pp. 20ff.

Cogan, J. (1982), 'The decline in black teenage employment: 1950-70,' *American Economic Review*, vol. 72, no. 4, pp. 621-38.

Coleman, L., and Cook, S. (1976), 'The failures of minority capitalism: the Edapco case,' *Phylon*, vol. 37, no. 1, pp. 44-58.

Conrad, D. (1965), *The Forgotten Farmer* (Urbana, Ill.: University of Illinois Press).

Corcoran, M., and Duncan, G. (1979), 'Work history, labor force

attachment, and earnings differences between the races and sexes,'
Journal of Human Resources, vol. 14, no. 1, pp. 1-20.

Cornish, D. (1968), 'Even the slave becomes a man,' in M. Drimmer (ed.), *Black History: a Reappraisal* (Garden City, NY: Doubleday), pp. 258-71.

Darity, W. (1982), 'The human capital approach to black-white earnings inequality: some unsettled questions,' *Journal of Human Resources*, vol. 17, no. 1, pp. 72-93.

Davis, A. (1941), *Deep South: A Social Anthropological Study of Caste and Class* (Chicago: University of Chicago Press).

Doeringer, P., and Piore, M. (1971), *Internal Labor Markets and Manpower Analysis* (Lexington, Mass.: Lexington Books).

Doeringer, P., and Piore, M. (1975), 'Unemployment and the "dual labor market",' *The Public Interest*, No. 38, Winter, pp. 67-79.

Doeringer, P., Piore, M., Feldman, P., Gordon, D., and Reich, M. (1972), *Low Income Labor Markets and Urban Manpower Programs: A Critical Assessment* (Washington, DC: US DOL, Research and Development Findings No. 12).

Dubois, W. E. B. (1899), *The Philadelphia Negro: A Social Study* (Philadelphia, Pa: University of Pennsylvania).

Dubois, W. E. B. (1964 [1935]), *Black Reconstruction in America: 1860-1880* (Cleveland, Ohio: Meridian Books).

Edwards, R. (1979), *Contested Terrain: The Transformation of the Workplace in the Twentieth Century* (New York: Basic Books).

Edwards, R., Reich, M., and Gordon, D. (eds.) (1975), *Labor Market Segmentation* (Lexington, Mass.: Lexington Books).

Epstein, G. (1986), 'What hath conservative economics wrought?' *Challenge*, vol. 29, no. 3, July/August, pp. 40-6.

Fatani, N. (1981), 'The transfer of technology and the technological gap between developed and less developed countries,' masters thesis, Atlanta University.

Feldstein, M. (1986), 'Supply-side economics: old truths and new claims,' *American Economic Review*, vol. 76, no. 2, pp. 26-30.

Foner, P. (1981), *Organized Labor and the Black Worker, 1619-1981* (New York: International Publications).

Frazier, E. F. (1957), *Black Bourgeoisie* (New York: Macmillan).

Freeman, R. (1976), *The Black Elite: The New Market for Highly Educated Black Americans* (New York: McGraw-Hill).

Friedman, M., and Friedman, R. (1980 [1979]), *Free to Choose: A Personal Statement* (New York: Harcourt Brace).

Giddens, A. (1973), *The Class Structure of Advanced Societies* (New York: Harper & Row).

Giddens, A., and Mackenzie, G. (eds.) (1982), *Social Class and the Division of Labour: Essays in Honour of Ilya Neustadt* (Cambridge: Cambridge University Press).

Gilder, G. (1981), *Wealth and Poverty* (New York: Basic Books).

Gordon, D., Edwards, R., and Reich, M. (1982), *Segmented Work, Divided Workers: The Historical Transformation of Labour in the United States* (Cambridge: Cambridge University Press).

Gouldner, A. (1979), *The Future of Intellectuals and the Rise of the New Class* (New York: Seabury).

Green, L., and Woodson, C. (1930), *The Negro Wage Earner* (New York: Association for the Study of Negro Life and History).

Greenwald, D. (ed.) (1982), *Encyclopedia of Economics* (New York: McGraw-Hill).

Hacker, Andrew (1979), 'Two "new classes" or none?' *Society*, vol. 16, no. 2, pp. 49-54.

Hailstone, T. (1982), *A Guide to Supply-Side Economics* (New York: Basic Books).

Harris, A. (1936), *The Negro as Capitalist* (Philadelphia, Pennsylvania: American Academy of Political and Social Science).

Harrison, B. (1972), *Education, Training, and the Urban Ghetto* (Baltimore, Md: Johns Hopkins University Press).

Harrison, B., and Sum, A. (1979), 'The theory of "dual" or segmented labor markets,' *Journal of Economic Issues*, vol. 13, no. 3, pp. 687-706.

Horowitz, I. (1979), 'On the expansion of new theories and the withering away of old classes,' *Society*, vol. 16, no. 2, pp. 55-62.

Johnson, C. (1970 [1943]), *Background to Patterns of Negro Segregation* (New York: Harper & Row).

Johnson, C., Embree, E., and Alexander, W. (1935), *Collapse of Cotton Tenancy* (Chapel Hill, NC: University of North Carolina).

Kalleberg, A., Wallace, M., and Althauser, R. (1981), 'Economic segmentation, worker power, and income inequality,' *American Journal of Sociology*, vol. 87, no. 3, pp. 651-83.

Kaplan, D. (1981), 'Reciprocity and commercialism,' *Society*, vol. 18, no. 6, September/October, pp. 51-5.

Keleher, R. (1981), 'Supply-side tax policy: reviewing the evidence,' *Economic Review*, vol. 66, no. 2, April (Atlanta, Ga: Federal Reserve Bank), pp. 16-21.

Keleher, R., and Orzechowski, W. (1981), 'Supply-side effects of fiscal policy: some historical perspectives,' *Economic Review*, vol. 66, no. 1, February (Atlanta, Ga: Federal Reserve Bank), pp. 26-8.

Kinsley, M. (1981), 'Tension and release,' *New Republic*, vol. 184, 7 February, pp. 25-31.

Konrad, G., and Szelenyi, I. (1979), *The Intellectuals on the Road to Class Power*, trans. A. Arato and R. Allen (New York: Harcourt Brace Jovanovich).

Kristol, I. (1978), *Two Cheers for Capitalism* (New York: Basic Books).

Kristol, I. (1981), 'A new look at capitalism,' *National Review*, vol. 33, no. 7, 17 April, pp. 414-15.

Laffer, A., and Conley, B. (1978), 'Interplay of taxes, output and fiscal policy,' *Tax Executive*, vol. 30, no. 4, pp. 336-43.

Landry, B. (1980), 'The social and economic adequacy of the black middle class,' in J. Washington (ed.), *Dilemmas of the New Black Middle Class* (Philadelphia, Pa: University of Pennsylvania Afro-American Studies Program), pp. 1-13.

Lenin, V. (1974), *Collected Works*, vol. 29 (Moscow: Progress Publishers).

Levitan, S., and Belous, R. (1979), 'The minimum wage today: how well does it work?' *Monthly Labor Review*, vol. 102, no. 7, July, pp. 17-21.

Liske, J. (1978), 'Conditions of racial violence in American cities: a developmental synthesis,' *American Political Science Review*, vol. 72, no. 4, pp. 1324-40.

Malcolm X (1965), *Malcolm X Speaks* (New York: Grove Press).

Marshall, R. (1974), 'The economics of racial discrimination: a survey,' *Journal of Economic Literature*, vol. 12, no. 3, pp. 849-71.

Marx, K. (1967), *Capital*, Vol. I (New York: International Publications).

Meir, A. (1968), 'Booker T. Washington: an interpretation,' in M. Drimmer (ed.), *Black History: A Reappraisal* (Garden City, NY: Doubleday) pp. 338-55.

Mieksins, P. (1981), 'Productive and unproductive labor and Marx's theory of class', *Review of Radical Political Economics*, vol. 13, no. 3, pp. 32-42. Mincer, J., and Polachek, S. (1974), 'Family investment in human capital: earnings of women,' *Journal of Political Economy*, vol. 82, no. 2, part II, pp. S76-S108.

Myrdal, G. (1944), *An American Dilemma: The Negro Problem and Modern Democracy* (New York: Harper & Row).

Oaxaca, R. (1973), 'Male-female wage differentials in urban labor markets,' *International Economic Review*, vol. 14, no. 3, pp. 693-709.

O'Connor, J. (1975), 'Productive and unproductive labor,' *Politics and Society*, vol. 5, no. 3, pp. 297-336.

Osborne, A., and Granfield, M. (1976), 'The potential of black capitalism in perspective,' *Public Policy*, vol. 24, no. 4, pp. 529-44.

Parkin, F. (1979), *Marxism and Class Theory: A Bourgeoisie Critique* (New York: Columbia University Press).

Pfautz, H. (1962), 'The power structure of the Negro subcommunity: a case study and a comparative view,'*Phylon*, vol. 23, no. 2, pp. 156-66.

Phelps, E. (1972), 'The statistical theory of racism and sexism,' *American Economic Review*, vol. 62, no. 4, pp. 659-61.

Pindyck, R., and Rubinfeld, D. (1981 [1976]), *Econometric Models and Economic Forecasts* (New York: McGraw-Hill).

Pinkney, A. (1984), *The Myth of Black Progress* (New York: Cambridge University Press).

Piore, M. (1969), 'On-the-job training in the dual labor market,' in A. Weber, F. Cassell and W. Ginsberg (eds.) *Public-Private Manpower Policies* (Madison, Wis.: Industrial Relations Research Association) pp. 101-32.

Piore, M. (1975), 'Notes on a theory of labor market stratification,' in Edwards, Reich and Gordon, op. cit., pp. 125-50.

Poulantzas, N. (1973), 'On social classes,' *New Left Review*, No. 78, pp. 27-54.

Poulantzas, N. (1975), *Classes in Contemporary Capitalism* (London: New Left Books).

Pryor, F. (1981), 'The "new class": analysis of the concept, the hypothesis and the idea as a research tool,' *American Journal of Economics and Sociology*, vol. 40, no. 4, pp. 367-80.

Rees, A. (1986), 'An essay on youth joblessness,' *Journal of Economic Literature*, vol. 24, no. 2, pp. 613-28.

Reich, M. (1981), *Racial Inequality: A Political Economic Analysis* (Princeton, NJ: Princeton University Press).

Reich, M. (1984), 'Segmented labour: time series hypothesis and evidence,' *Cambridge Journal of Economics*, vol. 8, no. 1, pp. 63-81.

Reich, M., Gordon, D., and Edwards, R. (1973), 'A theory of labor market segmentation,' *American Economic Review*, vol. 63, no. 3, pp. 359-65.

Resnick, S., and Wolff, R. (1982), 'Classes in Marxian theory,' *Review of Radical Political Economics*, vol. 13, no. 4, pp. 1-18.

Rosenberg, S. (1977), 'The Marxian reserve army of labor and the dual labor market,' *Politics and Society*, vol. 7, no. 2, pp. 221-8.

Ryan, P. (1981), 'Segmentation, duality and the internal labour market,' in F. Wilkinson (ed.), *The Dynamics of Labour Market Segmentation* (New York: Academic Press), pp. 3-20.

Schervish, P. (1983), *The Structural Determinants of Unemployment: Vulnerability and Power in Market Relations* (New York: Academic Press).

Sears, D., and McConahay, J. (1973), *The Politics of Violence* (Boston, Mass: Houghton Mifflin).

Sinclair, P. (1987), *Unemployment: Economic Theory and Evidence* (Oxford, UK: Basil Blackwell).

Singer, J. (1981a), 'A subminimum wage – jobs for youths or a break for their employers?' *National Journal*, vol. 13, no. 4, 24 January, pp. 146-8.

Singer, J. (1981), 'With a friend in the White House, black conservatives are speaking out,' *National Journal*, vol. 13, no. 11, 14 March, pp. 435-9.

Sowell, T. (1977), 'Minimum wage escalation,' (Stanford, Calif.: Hoover Institution Press), pp. 1-13.

Sowel, T. (1981), *Markets and Minorities* (New York: Basic Books).

Sowell, T. (1984), *Civil Rights: Rhetoric or Reality?* (New York: Morrow).

Spero, S., and Harris, A. (1972 [1931]), *The Black Worker: The Negro and the Labor Movement* (New York: Atheneum).

Stiglitz, J. (1973), 'Approaches to the economics of discrimination,' *American Economic Review*, vol. 63, no. 2, May, pp. 287-95.

Supel, T. (1980), 'Supply-side tax cuts: will they reduce inflation?' *Quarterly Review* (Federal Reserve Bank of Minnesota), vol. 4, no. 4, Fall, pp. 6-15.

Sweezy, P. (1953), *The Present as History: Essays and Reviews on Capitalism and Socialism* (New York: Monthly Review Press).

Todaro, M. (1982), *Economic Development in the Third World* (New York: Longman).

Toffler, A. (1980), *The Third Wave* (New York: Morrow).

US Department of Agriculture (1969; 1974), *Census of Agriculture* (Washington, DC: GPO).

US Department of Commerce, Bureau of the Census (1971), *Survey of Minority-Owned Businesses*, MB-1 (Washington, DC: GPO).

REFERENCES

US Department of Commerce, Bureau of the Census (1979), *The Social and Economic Status of the Black Population in the US: 1790-1978*, CPS Series p-23, No. 80 (Washington, DC: GPO).

US Department of Commerce, Bureau of the Census (1983), *America's Black Population: 1970 to 1982*, Special Publication PIO/POP-83-1 (Washington, DC: GPO).

US Department of Commerce, Bureau of the Census (1985), *1982 Survey of Minority-Owned Business Enterprises*, MB82-1 (Washington, DC: GPO).

US Department of Commerce, Bureau of the Census (1985), *Money and Poverty Status of Families and Persons in the United States: 1984* (Washington, DC: GPO).

US Department of Labor, Bureau of Labor Statistics (BLS) (1982), *Labor Force Statistics Derived from the Current Population Survey*, Vol. I, September (Washington, DC: GPO).

US Department of Labor, BLS (1983), *Job Tenure and Occupational Mobility* (Washington, DC: GPO).

US Department of Labor, BLS (1983; 1985; 1986), *Employment and Earnings*, January 1983, January 1985, February 1986 (Washington, DC: GPO).

US Department of Labor, BLS (1985), *Linking Employment Problems to Economic Status*, Bulletin 2222 (Washington, DC: GPO).

US Department of Labor, BLS (1987), *News*, USDL 87-44, 4 February (Washington, DC: GPO).

US Employment Service (1973-6 [1965]), *Dictionary of Occupational Titles* (Washington: US Government Printing Office).

US Small Business Administration (1984), *The State of Small Business* (Washington, DC: GPO).

Wachtel, H. (1975), 'Class consciousness and stratification in the labor process,' in Edwards, Reich and Gordon, op. cit., p. 95.

Wall Street Journal, 12 September 1986, pp. 1, 23.

Wallace, M., and Kalleberg, A. (1981), 'Economic organization of firms and labor market consequences: towards a specification of dual economy theory,' in I. Berg (ed.), *Sociological Perspectives on Labor Markets* (New York: Academic Press), pp. 77-117.

Wanniski, J. (1978), *The Way the World Works* (New York: Basic Books).

Weber, M. (1978), *Economy and Society*, Vol. 2 (Berkeley, Calif.: University of California Press).

Williams, R. (1962), *Negroes with Guns* (Chicago: Third World Press).

Williams, W. (1982a), 'On discrimination, prejudice, racial income differentials, and affirmative action,' in Block and Walker, op. cit., pp. 69-99.

Williams, W. (1982b), *The State against Blacks* (New York: New Press).

Wilson, W. J. (1978), *The Declining Significance of Race* (Chicago: University of Chicago Press).

Wright, E. (1978), *Class, Crisis and the State* (London: New Left Books).

Wright, E. (1979), *Class Structure and Income Determination* (New York: Academic Press)

Index

business enterprises
  black-owned 32–5
  changing organizational structures
    102
  factors affecting 37, 100
  minority, growth dynamics 36
  new black-owned 36, 37–8
  small middle class 39–41
capital
  as factor in business dynamics 37
  black access to 31
capitalist class 17
  old and new 17–18
  see also black capitalist class
capitalism, and supply-side economics
  140–1, 142
Civil Rights Act 1964 154, 155, 156
Civil Rights Movement 29, 37, 99
  conservative views of 154–5
  detrimental influences on black con-
    fidence 57
  impact of 155–7
  influence on black social class struc-
    tures 4, 5, 29, 37, 39, 41
  internal conflicts 45, 51–2
Civil War
  black participation 24
  impact on slavery 24
class consciousness 30, 41
  "grass-roots" 44
class theories
  of "new class" 13–15
  problems of definition and bound-
    aries 9–13, 16–20
congressional representation, black 25,
  26
conservative movement 46
  basic analysis of racial inequality 2–3,
    4, 8, 83, 154–5, 158–9
  effects of economic policies 153–4
  propositions concerning racial in-
    come inequality 54–8; lack of
    validation 59
  supply-side economic policy failure
    135–6, 151–2, 159
  views on labor market inequalities
    95–8
conservatives
  black 43–5, 156
  new black 4–5, 46, 152
costs, of discriminatory practices 2, 55,
  96
cotton production, and collapse of

black land tenancy 28
cultural differences, and income 56

discrimination, against women
  workers 74–8
  see also racial discrimination
domestic and personal service, antebellum period employment 26
Dubois, W.E.B. 44, 45

economic base, of new black-owned
  business 36
economic development, and class
  stratification 19
economic growth, major institutional
  changes 104–5
economic theory 136–8
  and class definition 9–11
  and elimination of poverty 135
  supply-side policies 94–5, 135–6,
    138–42, 159
education
  and income disparity 55, 59, 60,
    67–9
  as factor in business dynamics 37
employment
  declining employment status 146
  discriminatory practices 59, 72, 84,
    95
  during antebellum period 26
  in black-owned firms 35, 40
  opportunity inequalities 93, 114–15
  perceptions of worker productivity
    96–8
  self- 39
  see also labor
entrepreneurialism 38
  hostility from whites 40
ethnic factors
  as complication in class analyses 5
  in analysis of income inequalities 56,
    78
ethnic groups
  differential economic achievement
    56, 87
  non-political economic advancement
    152–3
  oppression and disadvantage 90–1

Fair Employment Practices Committee
  155
family
  race and income 144–5

169

INDEX

family *cont.*
size and income 78–80
Farrakan, L. 44
"field negroes" 51
financial institutions 31
see also banks
firm structures 102
job ladders 103
forced labor system 24, 98
Freedman's Savings and Trust
Company 31–2
free labor relations, 22, 23
free market system 154
and class status 3

geographic location, and income disparity 55, 69–71
"ghetto pathologies" 115
Gilder, G., supply-side economic theory 136, 138–42
government administrators, as the "new class" 13–14
government actions, as detrimental to racial advancement 56–7, 115
Great Britain, colonial government 99

human capital factors, in analysis of inequality 3, 4

incentives, in fiscal policy 138–40
income
effects of culture 56
in class classification and analyses 43
of small black-owned businesses 40
income inequality 3, 91
age and earnings differentials 63–7
conservative propositions on 54–8
educational attainment associations 67–9
family size determinants 78–80
feedback theories 115
of occupational categories 72–4
research variables and methodological problems 58–62
race and occupation differentials 142–4
sex and occupation variables 74–8
industrial development, and marginalization 49–50

Jackson, J. 44, 45
Jim Crow segregation 4, 25, 100
collapse 99
legally sanctioned 26, 98

Keynesian demand management economic policies 137–8, 142
King, M.L. 45
Ku Klux Klan 26

labor
black 114–15
dispossession in North 27
effects of discriminatory practices 55–6
"initial proletarianization" 104, 105
marginalized workers 48–50
middle class 42
secondary sector workers characteristics 116–17, 128–30
segmented 47–8
skilled 26, 39, 41
unemployed 133
unskilled 111
urbanized wage labor force 29
see also forced labor system; free labor relations
labor market
discrimination 58–9, 93
dual labor market theory 115–16
homogenization 104, 105
inequalities 93, 95
internal 102–3, 103–4
problems 146–7
segmentation 93, 104, 105–7, 116, 118; age distribution 127–8; identification by occupational characteristics 119–22; identifying boundaries 112–14, 116; position of black workers 114–15, 127; racial disproportions 122, 124, 125–7, 159
labor market segmentation theory
conservatism of 115–17
evolution of 101–4
research methodology problems 118
revised hypothesis 104–7; primary sector 107–9, 119, 121; secondary sector 109, 111–12, 113, 116–17, 119; weaknesses 116–17
labor unions 103
exclusion of blacks 27
land ownership, as accumulation of capital 31
legislation
civil rights 154, 155, 156
for forced labor system 24
restrictive labor 27
logit analysis 85–7, 122, 125–7

170